Parliament, Poli...
Issues and Developments in the
Legislative Process

Edited by Alex Brazier

Hansard Society
2004

Parliament, Politics and Law Making: Issues and Developments in the Legislative Process

Text and graphics © Hansard Society 2004

Published by the Hansard Society, 9 Kingsway, London, WC2B 6XF,
Tel: 0207 395 4000, Fax: 0207 395 4008

The Hansard Society is an independent, non-partisan educational charity, which exists to promote effective parliamentary democracy.

The Hansard Society's Parliament and Government Programme works on all issues relating to the reform of Parliament, engagement between Parliament and the public and promoting effective parliamentary government through a range of conferences, publications, public and private meetings.

We set the agenda on parliamentary reform through our work with parliamentarians and others to improve the operation of parliamentary government and encourage greater accessibility and closer engagement with the public.

For information about other Hansard Society publications visit our website at www.hansardsociety.org.uk

The views expressed in this publication are those of the authors. The Hansard Society, as an independent non-party organisation, is neither for nor against. The Society is, however, happy to publish these views and to invite analysis and discussion of them.

ISBN 0 900432 57 8

Printed and bound in Great Britain by Banjo Design and Print Ltd London SE15 1TF

Contents

Contributors to this publication

Alex Brazier is Senior Research Fellow on the Parliament and Government Programme, Hansard Society.

Paul Double was called to the Bar in 1981. He has been Remembrancer of the City of London and Parliamentary Law Officer of the Corporation of London since 2003. He has spent over 20 years in parliamentary legal work.

Clare Ettinghausen is the Director of Hansard Society.

Paul Evans is Head of the Scrutiny Unit in the House of Commons. Until October 2004 he was the Commons Clerk to the Joint Committee on Human Rights.

Neil Gerrard is Head of the Regulatory Group at the international law firm DLA.

Sam Hinton-Smith is an Account Manager at DLA Upstream, the government relations and strategic communications practice of DLA.

Vanessa Knapp is a partner in Freshfields Bruckhaus Deringer. She currently chairs the Law Society's Company Law Committee and is the UK representative of the Company Law Committee of the Council of the Bars and Law Societies of the European Union (CCBE).

David Lambert is a Solicitor and Notary Public and a Research Fellow in Public Law at Cardiff Law School. He and Marie Navarro are Senior Editors of the Law School's Digest of the powers of, and the law made by, the National Assembly for Wales. He has been Legal Adviser to the Welsh Office and to the Presiding Office of the National Assembly for Wales.

Dr Declan McHugh is Director of the Parliament and Government Programme, Hansard Society.

Marie Navarro has a Master of Law degree in International and European Law from the University Jules Verne of Picardy. She is a Research Associate at Cardiff Law School where she is studying for an M.Phil degree on the development of devolution in Wales.

Lord Norton of Louth [Philip Norton] is Professor of Government, and Director of the Centre for Legislative Studies, at the University of Hull. He chairs the Constitution Committee of the House of Lords.

Barry K. Winetrobe is a Lecturer in Public Law at Glasgow University, a member of the Hansard Society and its Scottish Working Group, and has worked in the Westminster and Scottish Parliament research services. He writes widely on parliamentary and constitutional issues.

Introduction

Clare Ettinghausen

The Hansard Society is an independent non-partisan organisation that works to promote effective parliamentary democracy. Our programmes of work span a wide range of activities designed to engage the public in the parliamentary and political process. We provide educational materials for all age groups and work with Parliament to improve its effectiveness.

The Hansard Society believes that an effective and well-functioning Parliament is essential to the health of democracy and has worked for over 60 years towards that end. The focus of this collection of essays is on the legislative process: reviewing developments in recent years; assessing the effectiveness of the current system and highlighting areas where improvements could be made.

In doing so, we are building on previous Hansard Society work on Parliament and the law making process, most notably the Commission on the Legislative Process, which reported in 1992, under the chairmanship of Lord Rippon of Hexham. The Commission looked at the law making process in its entirety and its report, *Making the Law*, is widely regarded as one of the most authoritative texts on the UK legislative process.[1] As the authors in this publication make clear, *Making the Law*'s analysis, conclusions and recommendations have proved extremely influential within Parliament and government, and many of the report's individual proposals have either been adopted, or have influenced the debate on the legislative process.

For example, pre-legislative scrutiny, one of *Making the Law*'s central recommendations, has become increasingly widely used in recent years, although as Alex Brazier notes, there is a long way to go before it is a standard part of the legislative process for all Bills. Likewise, the use of carry-over of Bills from one session to another is a further Commission proposal that has since been implemented. In many other areas, however, the system remains unchanged. Most notably, despite the introduction of programming of legislation, the organisation and timetabling of business in Parliament remains largely opaque and executive driven. As a consequence, calls for some form of legislation steering committee to deal with legislative matters in the Commons, as outlined in *Making the Law*, are repeated on these pages.

Yet, whilst many aspects of the legislative process in the Westminster Parliament have ostensibly been left untouched, the decade since *Making the Law* was published has witnessed profound political and constitutional changes that have impacted on governance across the UK. These include a change of government; devolution to Scotland, Wales and Northern Ireland; the implementation of the Maastricht and other European Treaties; and the increasing influence of human rights legislation. These changes, and many others that have occurred in the governance of the country, have all reshaped the political and constitutional landscape.

In view of the changed context, the Hansard Society decided, in 2003, that the time was right to reappraise the legislative process. Instead of revisiting the process as a whole, five important elements were identified to be the subject of briefing papers published in 2003-04.[2] The five briefing papers, sponsored by the international law firm DLA, looked at: Private Members' Bills, Standing Committees, Delegated Legislation, Programming of Legislation and Pre-legislative Scrutiny. This volume, *Parliament, Politics and Law Making*, brings together five chapters based on these topics, alongside additional essays looking at other aspects of the legislative process in the wake of constitutional changes since 1992.

Lord Norton of Louth opens the book with an overview of the legislative process, describing many of the changes that have been made and highlighting areas where the system could be improved. He focuses particularly on parliamentary scrutiny of public bills, identifying ways that Parliament can make a difference to the legislation it passes.

Alex Brazier then looks in detail at five key areas of the legislative process (outlined above), examining the impact of reforms and offering suggestions for further measures to improve the overall process. He shows that some of these areas, most notably the programming of legislation and pre-legislative scrutiny, have been the subject of significant procedural reforms, while others, primarily delegated legislation and Private Members' Bills, remain virtually unchanged in the decade since *Making the Law* was published.

Barry Winetrobe examines the impact of devolution by looking at the methods that the Scottish Parliament uses to consider legislation, contrasting them with the Westminster Parliament. David Lambert and Marie Navarro describe the very different procedures in place under the devolution settlement for Wales. Paul Double then provides an analysis of the growing impact of the European Union institutions on UK law and considers the implications for parliamentary scrutiny of European legislation.

Paul Evans uses his vantage point as former clerk of the Joint Committee on Human Rights to examine the impact of the Human Rights Act on the legislative process, while Neil Gerrard and Sam Hinton-Smith focus on the increasingly demanding nature of regulation and how this matches up to parliamentary scrutiny. Finally, Vanessa Knapp and Declan McHugh put legislative developments in recent years in the context of practice within and beyond Parliament, looking at how practitioners from both law and politics have managed these developments. Together these essays represent an important contribution for students, academics and practitioners to the debate on legislative reform.

Acknowledgements: This report and briefing papers have benefited from the generous support of the regulatory group of the international law firm DLA. The authors in this volume have been generous with their time and we are grateful for their contributions. Members of the Hansard Society Council have assisted with this research from the outset and have helped to guide it along the way.

Assistance has also been provided from a number of clerks and other experts within and outside Parliament and their help with factual and background information has been invaluable. We have worked closely with the Law Society's Better Law Making Programme throughout this series and are grateful for their help with this project.

Alex Brazier, Senior Research Fellow at the Hansard Society, has authored all five briefing papers and the resulting chapters, and has also edited this publication. There are a number of current and former members of Hansard Society staff who have assisted with this publication, Ross Ferguson, Virginia Gibbons, Caroline Gordon, Declan McHugh and Vidya Ram and interns who provided valuable research, Andrew Cork, Stephen Hartley, Michael Jacobs, Hannah Smith and Matthew Towey.

We hope that this publication contributes to the debate on reform of the law making process and stimulates discussion both within Parliament and government and also, crucially, in the wider world. The Hansard Society will continue to work with all those involved in this process and with members of the public to achieve ongoing reforms.

Clare Ettinghausen
Director, Hansard Society
December 2004

Endnotes and references:

1   *Making the Law:* The Report of the Hansard Society Commission on the Legislative Process, London: Hansard Society (1992).
2   Hansard Society Briefing Papers, Issues in Law Making: Paper 1: *Private Members' Bills,* May 2003, Paper 2: *Standing Committees,* July 2003, Paper 3: *Delegated Legislation,* December 2003, Paper 4: *Programming of Legislation,* April 2004, Paper 5: *Pre-legislative Scrutiny,* July 2004.

1 | Parliament and Legislative Scrutiny: An Overview of Issues in the Legislative Process

Lord Norton of Louth

Introduction: Acts of Parliament affect the shape and nature of British society. They shape behaviour. They stipulate what is permissible and, more pervasively, what is not permissible. They are enforced by agencies of the state, including the police and the courts. Their volume has grown enormously, with more being added year by year and with very few being repealed. There are few aspects of daily life that are not now affected by Acts of Parliament and by regulations made under those Acts. Acts of Parliament have made possible the enforcement in the United Kingdom of rules made by the supra-national institutions of the European Union. They have made possible the application of a mass of regulations by regulatory bodies within the United Kingdom. They have, over time, stipulated what is and what is not permissible in terms of private behaviour as well as public conduct.

Parliament's role in law making: Statute law is thus of fundamental importance. Acts of Parliament, as the name implies, create a role for Parliament that is intrinsic to the promulgation of law in the United Kingdom. However, that role is much misunderstood. It is common to refer to Parliament as a law making body, the body that puts together the measures that form the law of the land. The terminology is misleading and much confusion derives from it. Parliament is not a law making body. Law is generally 'made', that is formulated in a coherent form, by the executive, initially the Crown and now, in practice, the government. Parliament is more appropriately characterised as a *law effecting* body.

What defines Parliament as a legislature is the fact that its assent is required for a measure to become law, that is, an Act of Parliament. Conferring assent, on behalf of a wider community, to measures of public policy that are to have binding applicability within a society is what defines a legislature.[1]

Parliament's position as a legislature was established in the early centuries of its history but not confirmed until the Glorious Revolution of 1688 and the promulgation of the Bill of Rights in 1689. Even after the Glorious Revolution, those responsible for the Bill of Rights wanted, as Maitland recorded, 'a real, working, governing King, a King with a policy'.[2] The government brings forward measures of public policy, to which it seeks the assent of Parliament. However, assent is a function that defines, but does not confine, Parliament. That is, there is more to Parliament than simply the giving of assent. The fact that this assent may not be forthcoming – Parliament has the capacity to say no to government – gives Parliament leverage not only in relation to the content of the measures but also in relation to the actions of government.

Parliament may thus be described as a policy influencing rather than a policy making legislature.[3] That is, it does not have the capacity to formulate policy of its own and substitute it for that brought forward by government. Instead, it has the capacity to amend or reject the policy brought before it, but not to substitute a policy of its own. If it says no to government, it expects government to formulate a new policy of its own. The onus rests with government. Parliament, then, is important not only for giving assent to legislation but also for subjecting the measures laid before it to scrutiny. Other bodies may study and comment on proposals for legislation, but none has the constitutional authority for giving assent to it that Parliament has. That establishes Parliament's authority as the body for engaging in scrutiny, for satisfying itself that the measure is desirable in principle and embodies the most effective means for achieving that principle. Government may draw up the Bills but it is Parliament that has the responsibility for ensuring that they are appropriate and fit for purpose.

Given this responsibility, it is not surprising that Parliament accords considerable time to legislative scrutiny. Usually, about a third of the time of the House of Commons is given over to legislation, complemented by the time occupied by standing committees (of which, at busy times, there may be as many as eight operating simultaneously). In the Lords, the proportion of time is even greater – usually over 50 per cent – complemented now by the time spent by some Bills in Grand Committee. Time, however, is a necessary but not a sufficient condition for Parliament to engage in effective legislative scrutiny. It also needs the structures, resources and political will if it is to ensure that Bills are thoroughly scrutinised and bad law avoided. Critics have, for many decades, argued that in these respects the institution is deficient. L. S. Amery, in his *Thoughts on the Constitution* in 1947 declared that Parliament had 'become an overworked legislation factory'.[4] Almost 50 years later, the Hansard Commission on the Legislative Process, under Lord Rippon of Hexham (the Rippon Commission), came to a similar conclusion. In its report, *Making the Law*, it declared,

'There is undoubtedly widespread concern about the way the legislative process works and about its final product, statute law. For some time many of those who make the law, many of those who have to apply the law and many of those who have to comply with the law have been unhappy about the way legislation is prepared, drafted, passed through Parliament and published. All the evidence we have received bears this out.'[5]

It went on to list various bodies that had reported on the problem and made recommendations for change, noting, 'The sorry fact is that despite these critical but constructive reports almost nothing has been done to improve the situation.'[6] The Rippon Commission itself went on to make 111 recommendations for change.

What, then, has been achieved over the past decade or so? Are we any nearer to achieving an effective process of effective parliamentary scrutiny of Bills or does Parliament remain 'an overworked legislation factory'?

The Rippon Commission identified six stages of the legislative process: initiation, preparation, drafting, scrutiny and passage of Bills by both Houses of Parliament, publication of Acts, and post-legislative review. These can be subsumed into three basic stages: pre-legislative scrutiny, legislative scrutiny, and post-legislative scrutiny. The problems with parliamentary scrutiny can be viewed almost in ascending order. There have been marked advances in pre-legislative scrutiny, small but important changes in legislative scrutiny, but no changes in post-legislative scrutiny.

Pre-legislative scrutiny: Bills are drawn up by government. Ministers propose, the relevant cabinet committee agrees, the Legislative Programme Committee of the cabinet finds a slot in the legislative timetable, and parliamentary counsel draft the measure. It is then laid before Parliament for approval. This is one part of the process where considerable progress has been made. Parliament is no longer a total outsider, a body waiting until a Bill is laid before it. It now has an opportunity to influence legislation at a formative stage.

There have been two useful developments in the field of pre-legislative scrutiny. One has been the more extensive process of consultation on proposed measures. Green Papers and consultation papers now regularly emanate from government departments, working within a clear, and published, set of guidelines. Almost 80 per cent of consultations keep within the stipulated 12 weeks for comments from interested parties. Those parties may include parliamentarians and even parliamentary committees.

However, the most significant – and welcome – development from the perspective of Parliament has been the publication of Bills in draft. In other words, Bills are published ahead of their introduction to Parliament. This enables time for comments to be made before the measure is finalised and formally introduced. The practice of publishing Bills in draft developed under the Conservative Government of John Major and has been considerably expanded under the present government. Between 1992 and 1997, 18 Bills were published in draft, though not subject to systematic parliamentary consideration. In the seven sessions from 1997-98 to 2003-04 inclusively, no fewer than 42 Bills were published in draft. Most of these - 29 - have been subject to parliamentary scrutiny.[7] The mode of scrutiny has been by committee, but the type of committee has varied. Most - 17 - have been considered by departmental select committees in the Commons. Eight have been considered by joint committees of the two Houses, two by temporary committees in the Commons or Lords, and two by other existing committees.

The experience of the committees examining these Bills has generally been a productive one. Evidence given to the Constitution Committee in the House of Lords by parliamentarians involved in the joint committees indicated that the committees had proved to be a worthwhile and effective influence on the content of the Bills. The extent of the impact of parliamentary scrutiny is shown especially in the case of the joint committees on the Draft Communications Bill and the Draft Civil Contingencies Bill. In its response to the former committee, the government indicated that it had accepted 120 of its 148 recommendations. In its response to the latter Committee, it stated that, to a large extent, 'we have accepted in full, or in part, most of the recommendations'.[8]

The value of pre-legislative scrutiny by parliamentary committees is apparent. It enables Parliament to have an input at a formative stage, before the minds of ministers are set and before they have to get to the despatch box and defend publicly what the government has agreed. There is no need for each proposed amendment to be subject to a specific process of public debate, often in a partisan environment. This constructive input is facilitated by a structural element. Departmental select committees have developed some degree of bipartisanship in their approach to inquiries. Joint committees draw on Peers who may have some expertise in the field and who, in any event, are drawn from an environment less influenced by partisanship than the Commons. There is thus a presumption of a constructive approach to pre-legislative scrutiny.

The development of pre-legislative scrutiny may be seen as an unqualified good from the perspective of parliamentary scrutiny. However, it is far from problem free. The problem is not with the scrutiny that is undertaken but rather its limited application. Although the government has stated that the presumption should be that Bills would be published in draft unless there are good reasons for not doing so, it is still the case that only a minority of Bills are subject to pre-legislative scrutiny. As we have seen, not all Bills published in draft have been considered by parliamentary committees. One committee wanted to consider a draft Bill but was told that there was not time. One of the problems here is that Bills are often published in draft towards the end of a session, with a view to being introduced the following session. There is thus a remarkably limited window of opportunity for parliamentary scrutiny, and in some cases it is only as a result of Herculean efforts that joint committees have managed to report in time to influence the content of a Bill.

Crucially, the decision as to which Bills should be published in draft, whether or not they should be subject to parliamentary scrutiny, and, if so, by what form of committee, rests entirely with the government. There will be government resistance to any attempt by Parliament to have ownership of the process, but until Parliament is more centrally involved in deciding for itself what form the scrutiny should take then limitations will remain.

Legislative scrutiny: Once a Bill is introduced to Parliament, it goes through the established stages in both Houses. There are important differences, not least in terms of the time accorded legislation on the floor of the House in the Lords and the several stages at which amendments can be pursued; amendments in the Lords can be, and frequently are, taken at Third Reading. The Lords also has the advantage of not being constrained by programming motions or the selection of amendments. As a result, the House is able to devote most of its time to the detailed consideration of Bills.

There have been some constructive developments since *Making the Law* was published, developments very much in line with what the Rippon Commission advocated (if not necessarily envisaged). One has been in terms of what is brought before Parliament. Parliamentary counsel have made notable advances in ensuring that Bills are drafted in more accessible language that make them more understandable for parliamentarians and indeed the courts. Also, since the 1998-99 session, Bills have been accompanied by explanatory notes, which – while varying at times in quality of content – represent an invaluable aid to members of both Houses in making sense of what the provisions of a Bill are intended to achieve. The other principal change has been that both Houses in 2002 made provision for the carry-over of some Bills from one session to another. This was something recommended by the Rippon Commission and something in which I declare an interest. I recommended carry-over to the Commission and it was something to which I was able to return when chairing the Commission to Strengthen Parliament, which reported in 2000.[9] The idea was one taken up and endorsed by the new Leader of the House of Commons, Robin Cook MP, in 2001.

The case for carry-over is clear and ties in with enhancing not only scrutiny at this stage but at the pre-legislative stage. Allowing a Bill to carry-over from one session to another allows for the staggered introduction of Bills and for a more even distribution of parliamentary resources. It avoids what Robin Cook has characterised as the 'tidal wave' approach to legislation,[10] the government's Bills being introduced in one wave at the beginning of a session and then cascading down to standing committees later in the session (and to the House of Lords even later). It enables Parliament to give time for detailed scrutiny without having to be unnecessarily rushed to get through everything by the end of the session. It reduces the burden on parliamentary counsel, since all Bills do not need to be ready for early in the session, and it also facilitates pre-legislative scrutiny: the rush at the end of the session to engage in pre-legislative scrutiny, with a view to the Bill being introduced at the start of the new session, is avoided.

There is thus a powerful case for carry-over, though with some stipulated cut-off (say, 14 months after the Bill's introduction) to preserve discipline and allow some leverage for opposition parties. The problem to date has been the limited use of carry-over: only three Bills to date, with the Constitutional Reform Bill agreed to be carried over by the House of Lords from the 2003-04 session to the next. The 'tidal wave' mentality still predominates and as long as it does the pressures that generate rushed parliamentary scrutiny will remain.

The enduring problems of this stage include, rather centrally, standing committees in the Commons. (The operation of standing committees is discussed further in Chapter 2.) Apart from Bills taken in Committee of the Whole House, most Bills are referred to standing committees. In recent years, only the 1999 Immigration and Asylum Bill has been referred to a Special Standing Committee (SSC), which is empowered to take evidence prior to reverting to normal standing committee mode. The Rippon Commission recommended that Bills should be referred to SSCs as a matter of course. Three Bills have, though, been referred for consideration in select committees before being committed to a Committee of the Whole House (the 2001 Adoption and Children Bill, the 2001 Capital Allowances Bill, and the 2002 Tax (Earnings and Pensions) Bill). Regrettably, these are the exceptions and not the rule. Most Bills are considered in fairly sterile standing committees, with little being achieved in terms of sustained and constructive parliamentary scrutiny. The passage of Bills through the Commons, especially if subject to a tight programming motion, means that much legislation is inadequately considered (or not considered at all) by the Commons, leaving the Lords to ensure that all parts of the Bill are considered. This places a particular burden on Peers, and certain Peers – especially opposition frontbenchers – in particular.

There are thus major deficiencies with the process of parliamentary scrutiny of Bills, especially in the House of Commons. The Lords procedure – though not always appreciated by government – provides an essential means for ensuring that Bills are at least less bad than they otherwise would be. It is not, however, a failsafe device. Bad legislation still gets on to the statute book, but the statute book would be in a worse state than it is were it not for the House of Lords. It provides the means both for scrutiny and for second thoughts by the government itself.

Post-legislative scrutiny: This section need take up relatively little space for the depressing reason that the scrutiny is virtually non-existent and it attracts relatively little attention. Even the Rippon Commission, having identified questions to be asked through post-legislative scrutiny, failed to address how such scrutiny should be undertaken. Parliament tends to regard its duty as completed once a Bill has gone for Royal Assent, which is the very final stage of the law effecting process. Yet, as the Rippon Commission realised, there are questions to be asked about legislation once enacted: are the policies applied still desirable or acceptable; what problems have there been in interpreting, enforcing, administering and complying with the Act?[11]

At the moment, Parliament only becomes aware of problems either because of sporadic review, for example by a select committee, or because the legislation is seen to have dire and unintended effects. An obvious example of the latter is the Child Support Act 1991. The problems this Act generated contributed to pressure for improved legislative scrutiny, not least pre-legislative scrutiny, but did not lead to any systematic means of post-legislative scrutiny. Parliamentary scrutiny of the effects of legislation may enable problems to be identified early rather than when the negative consequences have become acute. Some measures in particular may lend themselves to review within two or three years of coming into effect. The 2001 Anti-Terrorism, Crime and Security Act did provide for post-legislative review, but in this case by a committee of Privy Councillors.

There is thus a powerful case for post-legislative scrutiny by Parliament, though, as with enhancing scrutiny at the other stages, it has obvious resource implications. Providing resources, including specialist support, though possible, is easier said than done. For resources to be provided, the political will has to exist to deliver them. Government may be sympathetic, but not necessarily sympathetic to the extent of agreeing changes that may delay its legislative programme or indeed subject it to sustained and possibly critical scrutiny. Ministers may at times be persuadable, but their departments may not. Parliament itself has to be willing to take ownership of the process and, in the House of Commons, that is a problem. Most MPs are elected to support and sustain the government. Those MPs are members of an institution that is expected to subject that very same government to critical scrutiny. When it comes to a case of party versus Parliament, partisan self-interest will not necessarily deliver a victory to Parliament. Achieving change is not simply identifying structures and processes, it is also a process of persuading MPs of the benefits – to them as well as to the House, and indeed government – of enhanced parliamentary scrutiny, resulting in legislation in the UK that is far more fit for purpose.

Conclusion: There are issues extending beyond the scrutiny of government Bills. There are the order-making powers embodied in them and later exercised by ministers. There are public Bills introduced by private members. The House of Lords has addressed the former through two committees. The Delegated Powers and Regulatory Reform Committee addresses the input side: the order making powers included in Bills. The newly appointed Select Committee on the Merits of Statutory Instruments addresses the output side: the actual orders made by ministers who are given powers by an Act. However, as with the legislative process, the positive developments have not yet kept pace with the complexity and sheer volume of the legislation involved. Private Members' Bills complete the family of public legislation and, on the face of it, comprise the one area where Parliament may claim to be a policy making, rather than a policy influencing, legislature. In practice, a substantial proportion of the legislation that makes it on to the statute book as Private Members' legislation comprises departmental handout Bills. Private Members' legislation thus comprises an additional channel for some departmental Bills. This is a problem as the value of debate on Bills that genuinely originate with MPs (or, in practice, organisations they sympathise with) is that it helps generate debate on what may be a matter of importance to particular groups in society.

The overall problems are with the scrutiny of government Bills, the measures once enacted and the orders made under them. Parliament has moved forward in a number of areas – notably in terms of pre-legislative scrutiny – but parliamentary scrutiny of public legislation remains limited, especially so in the House of Commons. Given the importance of Acts of Parliament to the life of the nation, and the activities of individual citizens, there is an imperative for Parliament to enhance its capacity for legislative scrutiny. That will only be achieved if Parliament wills it. There is a long way to go.

Endnotes and references:

1   See Norton P. 'General Introduction', in Norton P. (ed) *Legislatures*, Oxford: Oxford University Press (1990) p. 1.
2   Cited in Wiseman H. V. (ed) *Parliament and the Executive*, London: Routledge and Kegan Paul (1966) p. 5.
3   See Norton P. *Does Parliament Matter?* Hemel Hempstead: Harvester Wheatsheaf (1993) pp. 50-51.
4   Amery L. S. *Thoughts on the Constitution*, Oxford: Oxford University Press (1964) p. 41.
5   *Making the Law: The Report of the Hansard Society Commission on the Legislative Process*, London: Hansard Society (1992) p. 1.
6   *Making the Law*, p. 2.
7   Kennon A. 'Pre-legislative scrutiny of draft bills', *Public Law* (Autumn 2004) p. 478.
8   The Cabinet Office *The Government's Response to the Report of the Joint Committee on the Draft Civil Contingencies Bill* (January 2004) Cm 6078, p. 3.
9   *Strengthening Parliament: The Report of the Commission to Strengthen Parliament*, chaired by Lord Norton of Louth, Conservative Party: London (2000).
10 Robin Cook MP, *Point of Departure*, London: Simon and Schuster (2003) p. 11.
11 *Making the Law*, pp. 8-9.

2 | Standing Committees: Imperfect Scrutiny

Alex Brazier

Introduction: Standing committees (STCs) are temporary committees that are set up in the House of Commons to scrutinise a Bill in detail, following its Second Reading. They are a central part of the legislative process and enable backbench MPs to have a direct and detailed role in the legislative process. However, few aspects of the legislative process are as regularly, or as severely, criticised as STCs. They are variously regarded as delivering weak and incomplete scrutiny, allowing important parts of Bills to pass through unread and unconsidered or simply being a forum for a display of government domination over Parliament. Nevertheless, despite these criticisms, and despite the crucial role that they play in the passage of legislation, there is little evidence that STCs have improved their performance in recent years.

How standing committees work: After obtaining its Second Reading, a Bill is sent to an STC. It is then examined, in detail, by committee members, who can propose amendments to the Bill. The minister responsible for the Bill will then respond, explaining the reasons why the amendment should or should not be accepted. The amendment may then be put to a vote. The government often proposes amendments of its own, perhaps simply to clarify language but sometimes to make major changes. Government amendments are almost always accepted. Not every amendment is put to a vote: often the promoter will withdraw it if the minister promises to make necessary changes.

While STCs can make significant changes to a Bill, they cannot alter it in such a way that destroys its main principles, as agreed during the Second Reading debate. Bills may be amended further at Report Stage in the Commons or during the Bill's passage through the House of Lords. Most STC proceedings are now subject to programme motions that limit the amount of time that STCs can spend in examining a Bill. STCs do not exist in the House of Lords. Instead, 14 days after Second Reading the Bill proceeds to its Committee Stage, which is usually in a Committee of the Whole House, which examines it line by line.[1]

Scant praise; much criticism: Despite the pivotal role of STCs in the passage of legislation, they attract widespread, and often trenchant, criticism. For example, the Commons Modernisation Committee in 1997 described STCs as 'often ... devoted to political partisan debate rather than constructive and systematic scrutiny', adding, 'on Bills where policy differences are great, the role of government backbenchers on a standing committee has been primarily to remain silent and to vote as directed'.[2] Andrew Tyrie MP, in his critical study of Parliament, cited colleagues on both sides of the House who described STCs as 'desperate', 'dire' and a 'pointless ritual'.[3] Such criticisms are not new. Richard Crossman, a former Leader of the House of Commons, described STCs in his diaries as 'inane' and a 'waste of time'.[4] More recently, Peter Riddell argued that 'the system has been geared entirely to getting Bills through regardless of whether they are properly scrutinised. During the standing committee stage of line-by-line scrutiny government backbenchers are actively discouraged from participating lest their speeches delay progress on a Bill, so they can be seen doing their constituency correspondence, and depending on the season, their Christmas cards.' Riddell further noted that, 'the more important and controversial the Bill, the less likely is Parliament to play a creative part in its scrutiny. The result is a mass of hastily considered and badly drafted Bills, which later have to be revised'.[5]

So, do STCs deserve such an appalling press? It is during the STC stage that a Bill passing through the Commons is scrutinised in detail. STCs provide MPs with the opportunity to consider the precise meaning, powers and implications of a Bill. In theory, STCs can have considerable impact on the final content of legislation and it is commonplace for ministers to assert that any difficulties that have been identified (for example, in the Second Reading debate) can be considered during the detailed scrutiny of the STC stage. It is for these reasons that pressure groups and lobby organisations make considerable effort to influence STCs. In reality such effort is often wasted, as usually it is only amendments that are acceptable to the government which are passed.

As a basic model, it is sensible and practical for a relatively small group of legislators to spend many hours, over several weeks, examining the minutiae of a Bill's provisions. The proceedings of STCs are important in allowing MPs, and their parties, to place on the record their support or dissent for a particular provision. It allows MPs, and in particular the opposition, to put down a marker or prediction to which they may return in future. Indeed, on occasion, if STC members are well informed, given enough time, and if the minister taking through the Bill is prepared to engage in genuine debate, STCs are able to provide an effective form of scrutiny and can tease out the details of a Bill.

However, it is not uncommon for individual clauses, or even whole sections of a Bill, to pass through an STC without even being read, much less being subject to any detailed scrutiny. Take the example of the Criminal Justice Bill, published in November 2002. A Home Affairs Committee report on the Bill had stated, 'We have serious concerns about some of the provisions, which we believe will shift the balance too far towards the state'.[6] However, despite the importance of the Bill and the fact that it would directly affect the liberties of citizens, the STC proved unable to scrutinise all its provisions. The STC considering the Bill began its proceedings in December 2002, met on 32 occasions and reported to the House in March 2003. However, before Report Stage the government introduced significant additions to the Bill (almost 500 amendments and 28 new clauses),[7] which had not been considered by the STC. The government granted extra time for the Report Stage, and although this step did not appear to satisfy the critics, the Bill was given its Third Reading in May 2003 and sent to the House of Lords.[8]

The advent of programming: In 1997, the introduction of programming led to major changes in the operation of STCs. Programming was introduced, originally on an experimental and consensual basis, to create timetables for the passage of a Bill through an STC and to set an 'out-date' to determine when the Bill should finish its STC stage. However, it is now used for virtually all government Bills, and the idea that programming represents a consensual agreement between the parties has essentially been abandoned. One of programming's main limitations is that it is not always possible to anticipate accurately the time needed for adequate consideration of a Bill and, if the time runs out, parts of the Bill may receive no scrutiny at all. Furthermore, once STC proceedings have finished, the government can introduce new clauses that may be subject to little or no scrutiny by the Commons. (The issue of programming is discussed in more detail in the following chapter, *Programming: From Consensus to Controversy*.)

Government control and adversarial culture: At the heart of criticisms about STCs is the limited extent to which their scrutiny results in any significant changes to a Bill, which are not merely the result of changes in government policy. The government usually controls STCs through its in-built majority and exercises this control to resist all but the most innocuous amendments proposed by opposition parties. As the composition of an STC reflects the balance of parties in the House of Commons and, as the governing party usually has a majority, government amendments will almost certainly get passed whereas most opposition amendments will fail. Of course, it is understandable and legitimate for the government to do its best to secure passage of its legislation in the form it wishes, based on its mandate from the electorate. It is also entirely legitimate for the opposition to oppose it. However, these factors inhibit dispassionate analysis of the merits, meaning and implications of a Bill.

The adversarial nature of the Commons, and the over-riding assumption that members will support or oppose a Bill according to party loyalties (backed up as necessary by the power of the whips) dominates STC proceedings. MPs, for the most part, wish to remain loyal to their party and support its position on any given piece of legislation. However, MPs are also parliamentarians and, as such, have a duty to represent something rather more intangible, namely, the public interest. A survey undertaken by the Hansard Society Commission on Parliamentary Scrutiny, published in 2001, illustrated the nature of these, often conflicting, roles.[9] The survey found that more than 70 per cent of MPs regarded examining legislation as a 'very' or 'quite important' part of their work. When asked to describe their most important role, 13 per cent of MPs responded with examining legislation, compared to just 2 per cent who believed voting with their political party to be their most important role. (By far the most favoured response, holding the government to account, received 33 per cent.) Select committees have shown that it is possible for MPs to approach scrutiny and accountability issues in a somewhat more dispassionate and objective manner. Yet STCs, where the party imperative dominates all other considerations, tell a different story. STCs rarely approach Bills in this manner and it is for this reason that other forms of scrutiny (for example, pre-legislative scrutiny) are often considered to be more effective in looking at the detail and implications of a Bill.

Reforms to standing committees: In an attempt to address the perceived failings of STCs, a number of reforms have been proposed. Some proposals seek to effect a cultural change, for example, by re-ordering their appearance and layout to a round table model (as used by select committees) in contrast to the current adversarial set-up. Other suggestions, to simplify the procedures and language used, aim to make STCs more accessible. Furthermore, in order to improve the quality of the deliberations, it has been proposed that outside experts could be allowed to sit on committees to help MPs with legal or technical matters (but not be allowed to vote).

However, more fundamental changes are necessary if STCs are to carry out their work more effectively. For example, further consideration could be given to the *Making the Law* recommendation that if the government puts down significant new clauses or amendments at Report Stage, Bills should be re-committed to a Special Standing Committee for additional scrutiny.[10] Alternatively, the detailed scrutiny of the Bill could be split between a Committee of the Whole House and STCs. This possibility was raised in the 1997 Modernisation Committee report and used for Bills such as the Sexual Offences (Amendment) Act 2000. This procedure might allow for clauses requiring greater scrutiny and consideration to be considered in depth by an STC whereas other parts of the Bill, which required a lighter touch, could be detached from the rest of the Bill. Crucially, mechanisms should be introduced to ensure STCs actually do the job they are charged with doing; i.e. scrutinising the Bill in detail and in its entirety. The following chapter on programming outlines a number of proposals that might ensure, or at least increase the likelihood, that all clauses and schedules of a Bill are considered by an STC.

Introducing extra scrutiny: Another way to improve legislative scrutiny is to introduce other forms of parliamentary scrutiny, supported by expert advice, at an early stage of the legislative process. The most effective way to achieve this is through greater use of pre-legislative scrutiny and consideration of Bills in draft. Although there has been some welcome progress on this front, and the number of Bills subject to such scrutiny has increased, pre-legislative scrutiny of draft Bills is still the exception rather than the norm. A guarantee of pre-legislative scrutiny for all (or virtually all) Bills might be the way to introduce the detailed scrutiny currently lacking in STCs' consideration of the formal Bill. (Chapter 4, *Pre-legislative Scrutiny: A Positive Innovation*, looks at the development of pre-legislative scrutiny in greater detail.)

Special Standing Committees: Greater use of Special Standing Committees might also improve the overall picture. A Special Standing Committee (SSC) is a temporary committee that combines the functions of a select and standing committee. An SSC can hear oral evidence at up to three sittings within 28 days after the committal of the Bill. Written evidence may also be called for. At the conclusion of these proceedings, the committee reverts to working like any other STC. *Making the Law* recommended that Bills should be committed more regularly to an SSC and believed that this would allow for expert witnesses to be called, providing an additional forum for consideration and scrutiny. The Conservative Party's report, *Strengthening Parliament*, also recommended that following Second Reading, Bills should be referred to an SSC unless the House directs otherwise, thereby reversing the current relationship.[11] One possibility would be to obtain advanced agreement that SSCs (or other forms of close scrutiny by Committee) should be used where the Bill in question has particularly complicated technical or administrative issues. Recent candidates would be child support and tax and pension credits Bills where the legislation's success relies as much, and possibly more so, on the detail in the Bill as on the policy intentions underpinning it. However, despite the welter of positive recommendations concerning SSCs, few have been taken up and SSCs are very rarely used.

Different committee models: Westminster is unusual in that it has separate committees for its legislative functions (standing committees) and for its accountability of government functions (select committees). Many other legislatures, such as those in Scotland and most of Western Europe, have dual-purpose committees that combine standing and select committee functions on a permanent basis.[12] The report of the Hansard Society Commission on Parliamentary Scrutiny, *The Challenge for Parliament,* proposed the introduction of one or two dual-purpose committees, which would undertake both scrutiny and legislative functions, in the belief that the expertise developed by members would enhance the execution of both functions. The report proposed that these committees should be established on a pilot basis and their performance evaluated by the Liaison Committee, and that if they were considered to be successful, they should become more widespread. It also proposed the introduction of larger select committees working through a variety of sub-committees to carry out the different aspects of legislative and accountability duties.[13]

Conclusion: STCs are charged with looking at the detail of a Bill and therefore must take a large share of the responsibility for the resulting legislation. Despite widespread and often severe criticisms of the way that they operate, standing committees remain relatively unchanged. There are some positive examples of Bills being given close and genuine consideration and of STCs making a real difference to the Bill at hand. However, STCs' scrutiny is frequently patchy and haphazard; many clauses can pass through an STC without any scrutiny at all, even when the provisions are of major importance and might have direct effects on the financial well-being or the liberties of the public. These deficiencies in legislative scrutiny have been apparent for many years. Bernard Crick, writing in 1968, made observations which remain as true today,

'The whole legislative process is really like a great iceberg: only a tenth of it may appear above the surface ... Parliament ... spend[s] far too much time criticising the inevitable and far too little in examining the submerged processes of administration and influence from which the pinnacles of legislation emerge ... let alone what happens to them afterwards. But at the moment as usual we do not build enough new roads; we simply put up more warning signs.'[14]

There are a number of different ways in which changes to the operation of STCs could open up new avenues of legislative scrutiny. Obviously not all of them need to be unlocked for the same Bill. However, there should be an assumption that at least one other forum of detailed scrutiny should be used to help mitigate the inevitable adversarial approach to scrutiny displayed in STCs. It should be the responsibility of all MPs sitting on an STC, regardless of their political allegiance, to ensure that the legislation in question has been fully and effectively scrutinised and debated. Some essential questions should always be asked:

- is the proposed law as clear and unambiguous as possible?

- are the measures practical and likely to be administratively sound?

- what will be the law's consequences?

The potential list of issues is lengthy and will vary for each Bill. However, there should at least be some broad criteria and benchmarks for scrutinising legislation and these do not appear to exist at present. STCs are the forum where the real detail and impact of a Bill should be considered. It is, of course, important that the government is able to exercise its mandate from the people and get its legislation through the House. It is equally important that Parliament has the opportunity to scrutinise and consider effectively the provisions and implications of that proposed legislation. In that respect, STCs do not always fit the purpose.

Endnotes and references:

1   There are procedures that may replace the Committee of the Whole House, including a Grand Committee which works in the same way as a Committee of the Whole House (but no votes can be taken); a Public Bill Committee where a number of Peers are selected to conduct the Committee Stage of government Bills of a technical and non-controversial nature; and a Special Public Bill Committee, which is analogous to the Special Standing Committee procedure in the Commons.

2   Modernisation Committee, First Report (1997-98) *The Legislative Process*, HC 190.

3   Andrew Tyrie MP, *Mr Blair's Poodle, An Agenda for Reviving the House of Commons*, Centre for Policy Studies. (2000).

4   Crossman R. The Crossman Diaries, *The Diary of a Cabinet Minister, Volume 3, Secretary of State for Social Services 1968-70* (1977).

5   Riddell P. *Parliament Under Blair* London (2000).

6   Home Affairs Committee (2002-03) *Criminal Justice Bill* HC 83.

7   See HC Deb 20/5/03, vol 405, col 842-3.

8   See *Justice on Trial. The Commons must improve this Bill*, The Guardian, 19 May 2003 and complaints from MPs e.g. Graham Allen MP, David Heath MP, HC Deb 20/5/03, vol 405, col 842-3.

9   See *The Challenge for Parliament: Making Government Accountable*, Hansard Society Commission on Parliamentary Scrutiny, chaired by Lord Newton of Braintree (2001), Appendix 4.

10 *Making the Law: The Report of the Hansard Society Commission on the Legislative Process*, London: Hansard Society (1992).

11 *Strengthening Parliament: The Report of the Commission to Strengthen Parliament*, chaired by Lord Norton of Louth, Conservative Party: London (2000).

12 The Scottish Parliament's subject committees deal with a particular subject of public policy and combine the functions of Westminster's select and standing committees. They can also initiate their own legislation.

13 *The Challenge for Parliament: Making Government Accountable*, Hansard Society Commission on Parliamentary Scrutiny, chaired by Lord Newton of Braintree (2001).

14 Crick B. *Reform of Parliament* London: Weidenfield & Nicolson (1968).

3 | Programming of Legislation: From Consensus to Controversy

Alex Brazier

Introduction: The previous chapter looked at the operation of standing committees. This chapter considers programming (or timetabling) of legislation, a development that has had a major impact on the way that standing committees operate and which has also had major implications on the wider legislative and parliamentary process. The Procedure Committee has described the introduction of programming as 'the most significant change for some years in the way the House considers Bills'.[1] Most government Bills are now subject to a form of programming in the House of Commons. Programming, on the basis of cross-party agreement, was originally introduced by the incoming Labour Government in 1997-98, with the intention of creating a more consensual legislative process. It was hoped that it would allow more effective and consistent scrutiny of proposed legislation while recognising both the need for the government to get its legislation through, and the opposition to hold debates and votes on the parts of a Bill that it considered important. However, the consensual nature of the programming agreements has since broken down and, according to some critics, programming has resulted in greater executive dominance over the legislature.

What is programming? Before 1998, there were two ways in which the House of Commons could timetable the various stages of a Bill. The first was informal timetabling when government and opposition business managers and whips - through a system known as the 'usual channels' - agreed a timetable for the passage of a particular piece of legislation.[2] The second method involved 'guillotine' motions, which were instigated by the government to curtail the time spent on Bills. Guillotines were usually moved when the government had been unable to reach voluntary agreements or when the opposition engaged in what the government perceived to be 'blocking' tactics.

Since 1998, programme motions have been introduced into the House of Commons (but not the House of Lords) to specify the amount of time that will be spent on a Bill. Programme motions are moved after a Bill's Second Reading and outline the timetable for future stages in the Commons. Crucially, programme motions specify a date by which proceedings in a standing committee must be concluded. They specify the number of days on the floor of the House reserved for the Report Stage and Third Reading, but do not specify the actual dates for those proceedings.

Before the first meeting of a standing committee, a programming sub-committee meets to make proposals about sitting times and the internal division of time within the parameters already decided by the government (i.e. the date of the first meeting and the 'out-date', when the Bill must leave the standing committee). The sub-committee can propose 'internal knives' which are the times at which proceedings to a certain point in the Bill must be concluded. The end of the time allocated for a certain part of the Bill is known, informally, as the point when the 'knife' falls. Any clauses not dealt with before the knife falls are effectively lost. The initial proposals from the sub-committee almost always reflect the government's view on how time should be divided. The programming sub-committee may make recommendations about a change to the 'out-date' or the programming of the Report Stage and Third Reading. However, in general, the sub-committee's decisions rarely do more than endorse formally what the government agrees to. Guillotines are now rarely used, only being enforced when the government wishes to programme all stages of a Bill.

The introduction of programming: Proposals for the introduction of some form of programming have been made for many years. For example, in 1985 the Procedure Committee recommended the creation of a Legislative Business Committee, to allocate time for a Bill's passage, citing a survey that suggested nearly three-quarters of MPs supported its introduction.[3] In 1992 the Report of the Select Committee on Sittings of the House, (known as 'The Jopling Report'), recommended that timetabling should be applied to all stages of government Bills after Second Reading.[4] Although many other Jopling proposals were adopted in 1995, the programming of public Bills was not implemented. During the 1992-97 Parliament, the Procedure Committee made further recommendations on programming but no action was taken. In 1992, *Making the Law* recommended the establishment of a Legislation Steering Committee to organise the shape of the legislative programme and deal with matters such as programming.[5] The report argued that by formalising the opposition's role in decision-making on the legislative process, it would not lose out if programming became widely used.

Given the breadth and frequency of such proposals, it is perhaps not surprising that one of the first actions of the Commons Modernisation Committee after the 1997 general election was to recommend the introduction of programming. The Committee described programming as 'more formal' than the usual channels but 'more flexible than the guillotine'.[6] The first programme motion, moved in January 1998 for the Scotland Bill, was hailed as the 'first ever all-party programme motion'.[7] During the period 1997-2000, however, programming motions were not frequently used. Only after new orders on programme motions were passed in 2000 and 2001, which gave more powers to programming committees and programming sub-committees, did the number of Bills subject to programming subsequently increase. By the 2000-01 session almost all government Bills were programmed, a situation which continues today.

Three distinct stages: Since 1997 the programming of legislation has gone through three distinct stages. The first phase was programming with cross-party agreement. In the period following the 1997 general election, the main opposition parties gave programming their support and the initial proposals in the 1997 Modernisation Committee report were passed unanimously. Although the opposition was not overly enthusiastic about programming, it felt that it might at least bring more certainty to the legislative process and would perhaps allow more time for developments such as pre-legislative scrutiny. This phase of programming essentially ended because agreement could not be reached after the initial consensus broke down. The Procedure Committee has cited a range of somewhat conflicting views to account for this breakdown. For example, Graham Allen MP ascribed the breakdown to a lack of willingness by the opposition whips to negotiate on the timetable within an overall limit; Sir George Young MP believed it was due to a lack of agreement on the 'out-date' from standing committee. Oliver Heald MP considered that 'the government refused sensible requests for flexibility and ended up guillotining everything ... every time we could not reach agreement we got guillotined'.[8] Overall, the opposition had become increasingly unhappy with the way programming worked in practice and came to regard it as a mechanism for the government to get its legislation passed more easily.

The second phase, from the 1999-2000 session onwards, was characterised by programme motions, which were non-consensual, though debatable. The motions were essentially carried by the votes of the government party against the wishes of the opposition. The third and current phase, involves programme motions, which are generally not debated. As far as critics of the system are concerned, the 'out-dates' simply represent the government's decision on how long the committee stage should take. Many within the opposition parties consider that programming has further diminished their influence over the legislative process and has delivered yet more power to the government. The result is that the initial intention that programming should represent the outcome of negotiations between parties, appears to have been abandoned.

Programming in practice: The tensions between oppositionalism and effective scrutiny, and between duties to Parliament versus partisanship, have had an enormous impact on programming in practice. The opposition routinely votes against programme motions and the government imposes its programming orders through the use of its majority. According to Blackburn and Kennon, 'there is a suspicion that this important procedural innovation has fallen foul of party politicking'.[9] Furthermore, there are concerns that the system of programming is flawed in its operation.

Programming was intended to eradicate, or at least greatly reduce, the gaps in scrutiny which occurred when time on a Bill ran out, resulting in many important clauses being left undebated. Although programming is meant to be flexible, it is not always possible to predict in advance the time that will be needed to give full consideration to parts of the Bill or predict which clauses will attract most attention or controversy. For example, in the 2002-03 session, 23 government Bills were subject to a programme order; in six cases, the committee ran ahead of timetable; in the remaining 17 cases the 'knives' fell leaving entire clauses and schedules undebated. In a number of cases, significant parts of the Bill received no scrutiny at all.[10]

And yet, despite the controversies and difficulties, programming has brought greater certainty, even rationality, to a legislative process that could previously appear bizarre and unpredictable. Some observers believe that standing committee proceedings have become more brisk and businesslike in recent years, partly because of programming. In the past, standing committees were characterised by a culture of late hours and long debates, often for their own sake. Since in a programmed system, filibustering and delay simply reduce the time available for constructive debate, programming may discourage such practices.

On the other hand, some participants in the system regard programming as having removed one of the few weapons that Parliament, or more specifically the opposition, had at its disposal in highlighting concerns about government legislative proposals. Without a programme in place, there was some scope for use of the 'time weapon' to cause inconvenience and perhaps even delay to the government's legislation. *Making the Law* was not convinced by this argument, pointing out that the 'so-called time weapon' led to 'long, boring, time-wasting filibusters' and eventually to the use of the guillotine which resulted in many parts of a Bill escaping all scrutiny and debate. Undoubtedly, the time weapon was blunt and ineffective; ultimately, the government's use of its majority and, where necessary, the use of the guillotine, meant it was certain of getting its legislation through. Nonetheless, according to the critics of programming, even if this weapon has obvious limitations, it at least provided some power, which is no longer available.

Proposals for change: Programming appears to be here to stay. However, there are many commentators who take the view that it is not working effectively. Consequently, there have been numerous calls for reform. One core reform, which might place programming in a wider context of reform, is the introduction of a business committee or legislation steering committee, which would allow greater input and agreement between all interested parties in the Commons about the shape and timing of the legislative programme, including programming.[11] Although there are different views about how a business committee might work in practice, such an innovation would allow opposition and backbench concerns to be raised in a formal setting and might make the overall process more straightforward and transparent. This was the position taken in *Making the Law* which argued that programming should be seen in the context of other, linked, changes to the legislative process, such as greater use of pre-legislative scrutiny and the introduction of carry-over of legislation. To some extent, it regarded programming as a means to a greater end and argued,

'It would be difficult for the Government's business managers to accept some of our recommendations for more effective scrutiny of Bills unless there were some compensating assurance, through time-tabling, that these would not cause unacceptable delays in the passage of legislation.'[12]

In the absence of a business committee, one option for reform would be to link the application of programming more explicitly to other reforms of the legislative process. For example, programme motions might only be moved immediately after Second Reading without debate if at least one of the following four conditions had been met:

(i)   the Bill had been subject to pre-legislative scrutiny;
(ii)   the Bill is to be subject to carry-over between sessions (to increase the overall time for scrutiny);
(iii)   the Bill is to be committed to a Committee of the Whole House or a Special Standing Committee;
(iv)   there is cross-party agreement on the terms of the programme.

In 2000, in *Mr Blair's Poodle*, Andrew Tyrie MP advocated that timetabling should be applied to all stages of a Bill.[13] However, he recognised that removing the margin of uncertainty for unprogrammed Bills would benefit the government, and believed that the executive should not gain something for nothing. He argued that the minimum trade-off for timetabling should be thorough pre-legislative scrutiny of Bills by select committees, reform of standing committees and a commitment that after a certain point, major government amendments, fundamentally altering the Bill, should not be allowed. One possibility would be for the Speaker to have the power to rule on whether a Bill had been so altered that it could be returned for another Second Reading. In particular, Tyrie identified an important role for select committees in taking evidence from ministers and expert parties (along the lines of a Special Standing Committee), to identify the clauses that appear straightforward and uncontenious and, conversely, to identify those parts of the Bill that need closer consideration and scrutiny.

Another possibility is that the government could be prohibited from moving a programme motion until after a standing committee had sat for four sitting days and such subsequent motions would also be debatable. The government would then at least need to make the case publicly as to why proceedings were not progressing adequately without a programme being in place. Another suggestion would be to make provision for 'injury time' in standing committee, specifically to debate the most important provisions lost to earlier 'internal knives'.

In 2003, the Modernisation Committee report, *Programming of Bills*, put forward a number of further recommendations, including that where large numbers of late amendments are tabled, the programming sub-committee should propose a revised out-date, which the government should support.[14] It also proposed that in the case of lengthy Bills, the programming sub-committee should not normally make detailed proposals about the allocation of time to the Bill until after several sittings of the standing committee, and should keep the operation of the 'knives' under careful review and that long delays between the out-date and Report Stage should be avoided.[15]

In July 2004, the House of Commons Procedure Committee published a major report of its inquiry into the programming of legislation.[16] It noted that since the demise of any cross-party agreement, programming has come to be seen in the same light as the guillotine. The report recommended that programming motions should be decided without debate only where there is cross-party support, otherwise the government should justify its position with a one-hour debate. In return it urged all parties to adopt a constructive approach to programming. Furthermore, it recommended that the initial programme motion for a Bill should be taken not less than 48 hours after Second Reading, to allow the proposed date for the end of committee stage to take account of the Second Reading debate and any representations made. For Report Stage and Third Reading it recommended that the government should table its amendments in good time and that the House should be provided with a factual statement of which clauses and schedules were not considered in committee because of the operation of the programme.

In October 2004 the government's reply to the Procedure Committee's report on programming was published.[17] The government accepted some of the recommendations made by the Procedure Committee, including that it would make efforts to reduce the number of internal knives and also to allow standing committees to vary the programme without the need for the programming sub-committee to meet (as long as there were no objections). However, it did not accept the proposal that programme motions should only be decided without debate if there was cross-party support for the motion, or, if such support was not forthcoming, that the government would have to justify the motion in a one-hour debate. Also, the government did not accept the Committee's proposal for the production of a factual statement of the clauses and schedules that had not been considered in committee to demonstrate to MPs, who had not been on the standing committee, which parts had not been debated. Subsequently, also in

October 2004, the government introduced changes to Commons Standing Orders which had the effect of making permanent the basic system of programming in operation since 2001.[18]

Conclusion: Timetabling of legislation has been supported by reformers of all political complexions for many years as a means to achieve the objective of rational, measured and full consideration of proposed legislation. It is clear that the fundamental bargain which needs to be struck is that the gain of greater certainty about the government's legislative timetable should be balanced against the opportunity for less rushed, more thorough, and more effective scrutiny.

Programming cannot be seen in isolation. Proposals for a business committee to organise parliamentary business, including the timetabling of legislation, are particularly relevant and should be revisited. Increased use of draft Bills, the regular use of Special Standing Committees, which can take evidence, and the provision of adequate time for Report Stages on the floor of the House should accompany the development of timetabling. To be fully successful, programming should become part of a package with reform measures. The Modernisation Committee identified the criteria for an effective legislative process in its 1997 report:

- the government of the day must be assured of getting its legislation through in reasonable time (provided that it obtains the approval of the House);

- the opposition, in particular, and Members in general must have a full opportunity to discuss and seek to change provisions to which they attach importance;

- all parts of a Bill must be properly considered.[19]

These are the criteria to which the legislative process should aspire. Yet many Bills are still subject to partial and inconsistent scrutiny. Of course, it should be acknowledged, as the Leader of the House of Commons, Peter Hain MP has pointed out, 'there was never a golden age of scrutiny of all Bills, every clause in every Bill'.[20] As the Modernisation Committee's 2003 report stated, 'on the contrary, prior to the introduction of programming, there was deep and widespread dissatisfaction with the haphazard nature of scrutiny', which had led to proposals for various types of timetabling.[21]

Nonetheless, a genuinely effective legislative process should not allow such gaps in consideration. The true test of the value of programming is, therefore, whether it helps restore Parliament's active participation in the making of law, rather than representing another mechanism that ensures that the government gets its legislation through the House.

Endnotes and references:

1 Procedure Committee (2003-04) *Programming of Legislation,* HC 325.
2 See Rush M., Ettinghausen C. *Opening Up The Usual Channels,* Hansard Society (2002).
3 Procedure Committee (1984-85), *Public Bill Procedure,* HC 49.
4 Report from the Select Committee on Sittings of the House (1991-92) HC 20.
5 *Making the Law: The Report of the Hansard Society Commission on the Legislative Process,* London: Hansard Society (1992).
6 Modernisation Committee (1997-98) *The Legislative Process,* HC 190.
7 Cabinet Office Press Notice (13/1/98).
8 See Procedure Committee (2003-04) *Programming of Legislation,* HC 325.
9 Blackburn R. and Kennon A. *Parliament, Functions, Practice and Procedures* London (2003).
10 The Modernisation Committee report (2002-03) *Programming of Bills,* HC 1222, identified the Planning and Compulsory Purchase Bill in 2002-03 as an example of where programming had not worked well; many clauses were not scrutinised at all. In the previous session, the opposition also criticised the timetables put into place, particularly those for the Enterprise Bill, which had resulted in a lack of time to scrutinise a significant portion of its provisions; see HC Deb 13/6/02, vol 368, col 1033.
11 *The Challenge for Parliament: Making Government Accountable,* Hansard Society Commission on Parliamentary Scrutiny, chaired by Lord Newton of Braintree (2001) also recommended the introduction of a business committee.
12 *Making the Law: The Report of the Hansard Society Commission on the Legislative Process,* London: Hansard Society (1992), para 81.
13 Andrew Tyrie MP *Mr Blair's Poodle, An agenda for reviving the House of Commons,* Centre for Policy Studies (2000).
14 Modernisation Committee (2002-03) *Programming of Bills,* HC 1222.
15 Generally Report Stage and Third Reading are completed on a single day but the complexity of some Bills may mean that two days (or more) may be required.
16 Procedure Committee (2003-04) *Programming of Legislation,* HC 325.
17 Procedure Committee (2003-04) *The Government's Response to the Committee's Fourth Report,* HC 1169.
18 See HC Deb 26/10/04, vol 425 col 1308-1407.
19 Modernisation Committee (1997-98) *The Legislative Process,* HC 190.
20 Procedure Committee (2003-04) *Programming of Legislation,* HC 325.
21 Modernisation Committee (2002-03) *Programming of Bills,* HC 1222.

4 | Pre-legislative Scrutiny: A Positive Innovation

Alex Brazier

Introduction: One of the most significant and positive developments in legislative reform in recent years has been the marked increase in pre-legislative scrutiny. Such scrutiny can allow for more measured consideration of a Bill's principles, questioning of new policy initiatives contained within it and consideration of any practical or technical issues which might arise from the proposed provisions. Pre-legislative scrutiny can utilise expert evidence and provide a forum for a wide range of interested parties to influence legislation at an early stage. It also provides an important mechanism for collaboration between the executive, legislature and electorate.

Most crucially, as ministers tend to commit less political capital to draft legislation than to formal legislation, they do not necessarily regard making changes to a draft Bill as a defeat. It may even be considered more advantageous to ministers if their draft legislation is altered at this stage, to permit smoother passage in the formal legislative process. This chapter looks at the development of pre-legislative scrutiny and considers ways that its development may further strengthen the way that Parliament makes the law.

What is pre-legislative scrutiny? Prior to a government Bill being formally published in final form, it may be published in draft. Since 1997, an increasing number of draft Bills have been referred to a parliamentary committee for pre-legislative scrutiny. Most draft Bills are referred to a Commons departmental select committee or a joint committee of both the Commons and the Lords. The government will publish a list of Bills that will be considered in pre-legislative form at the beginning of each parliamentary session. Those Bills put forward in draft form are done so at the discretion of the government's business managers. At present, only a relatively small (but growing) proportion of government Bills are subject to pre-legislative scrutiny.

When considering legislation in draft form, select committees are able to call witnesses for oral evidence and take written evidence from external sources.

Select committees are then able to report their findings in detail and explain why they either support or oppose the proposed Bill and explain the amendments that they deem appropriate. The government is not obliged to accept the alterations from the Committee, but in many cases, it has done so. As well as the particular provisions of the Bill, pre-legislative scrutiny can also consider the human rights implications, spending implications and delegated powers related to the Bill.

From proposals to implementation: The Hansard Society has long advocated the use of pre-legislative scrutiny; its *Making the Law* report stating that,

'There should be as full consultation as is practicable on draft bills and clauses... We therefore recommend that departments should offer more consultations on draft texts, especially in so far as they relate to practical questions of the implementation and enforcement of legislation ... Parliament could play a greater part by pre-legislative inquiry in the preparation of legislation.'[1]

Making the Law noted that very few pre-legislative inquiries on draft Bills had, at that point, been undertaken by select committees or other parliamentary forums, although it had not been unusual for select committees to hold inquiries on Green and White Papers or other consultative documents. Such inquiries allowed evidence taking and deliberation on broad principles, but were usually unable to focus on the specific, legally expressed, proposals that the government was intending to bring forward. During the 1992-97 Parliament, the Conservative Government published a number of Bills in draft for consultation purposes but they were not subject to formal scrutiny by parliamentary committees. The major step forward came with the Modernisation Committee's report in 1997, which concluded,

'There is almost universal agreement that pre-legislative scrutiny is right in principle, subject to the circumstances and nature of the legislation. It provides an opportunity for the House as a whole, for individual backbenchers, and for the Opposition to have a real input into the form of the actual legislation which subsequently emerges, not least because Ministers are likely to be far more receptive to suggestions for change before the Bill is actually published... Above all, it should lead to better legislation and less likelihood of subsequent amending legislation.'[2]

Since 1997, there has been a significant increase in pre-legislative scrutiny. Between the 1997-98 and 2003-04 parliamentary sessions a total of 42 draft Bills were published.[3] To help to consolidate the process, in May 2002 the Commons adopted guidelines for core functions and duties to be carried out by select committees, including 'to conduct scrutiny of any published draft Bill within the committee's responsibilities'.

Decisions and methods: The decision whether to publish a draft Bill, and to which committee it should be sent, is made entirely at the discretion of the government. There are no formal guidelines that indicate the sort of Bills that should be subject to pre-legislative scrutiny, or indicate whether a House of Commons select committee or a joint committee of both Houses should be chosen as the most appropriate forum. There is, however, a general presumption that a draft Bill will be scrutinised by the relevant Commons select committee. Nonetheless, the regular use of joint committees of both Houses shows that there are exceptions to this rule. Furthermore, other options have been used, including combined sub-committees of two or more departmental select committees in the Commons or an existing joint committee (e.g. the Joint Committee on Human Rights).

Departmental select committees undertaking pre-legislative scrutiny are generally able to establish their own terms of reference and methods of working for the inquiry, though they may be under some time constraint. There is no agreed formal procedure and this means that committees are able to concentrate on what they believe to be the most important parts of a Bill, whether they are principles or individual clauses. On the other hand, the motions establishing joint committees of both Houses include their terms of reference, which almost always includes a deadline by which time they should report.

The impact of pre-legislative scrutiny: Unlike standing committees, which have powers to change a Bill, committees looking at a draft Bill make recommendations that the government is at liberty to accept or reject. One obvious method to judge the impact of pre-legislative scrutiny is to assess which of the committee's recommendations have been accepted. In many cases it is obvious that the committee has had a significant impact and that the government has accepted the committee's proposals, either in spirit or to the letter. For example, the government accepted 120 of the 148 recommendations made by the joint committee looking at the draft Communications Bill in 2002.

Pre-legislative scrutiny can have other important effects. For example, it can stimulate and assist public and media debate on a subject. It can also provide a mechanism for pressure and lobby groups to campaign on an issue and to provide evidence to the committee and the House as a whole. Another important benefit is that members of the committee that conducted the inquiry will become better informed about the Bill and the issues that it addresses. Therefore, they are able to make more expert contributions when the formal Bill is introduced, whether in standing committee or in the chamber, thus raising the quality of debate and scrutiny.

From the government's point of view, draft Bills can be used as a 'consolation prize' if there is no room in the main legislative programme for a formal Bill. This may build up sufficient momentum to ensure the introduction of a Bill in the following session. Pre-legislative scrutiny has, to date, tended to be carried out on uncontroversial Bills (at least those Bills considered uncontroversial in party political terms). The Constitutional Reform Bill is an example of a politically controversial Bill which did not have pre-legislative scrutiny built into the process. In fact, the Commons Constitutional Affairs Committee believed it was a clear candidate for pre-legislative scrutiny and that 'draft Bills are appropriate whenever there is any significant proposal, which is complex, introduces fundamental change and is controversial'.[4] In the event, the House of Lords referred the Bill to a Special Select Committee, which was formed specifically to undertake further scrutiny.

Connecting with the public: The Modernisation Committee's 1997 report stated that pre-legislative scrutiny 'opens Parliament up to those outside affected by legislation'. It does this by offering scope for involving a greater number of people in the legislative process. There are numerous benefits to this: legislators can canvass a sense of public opinion around an issue and utilise the expertise and experience of relevant organisations and individuals to assess potential consequences. Being involved in the formal process of pre-legislative scrutiny can also improve Parliament's relationship with the public.

Proposals for change: A number of reports have recommended that pre-legislative scrutiny should be more frequently used and made more effective. In 2000, the Conservative Party report, *Strengthening Parliament*, recommended that the publication of draft Bills should become the norm, not the exception.[5] In 2002, the Modernisation Committee returned to the subject of pre-legislative scrutiny, stating that 'we hope eventually to see publication in draft become the norm. We recommend that the government continue to increase with each session the proportion of Bills published in draft.'[6] More recently, Phil Woolas MP, Deputy Leader of the House of Commons, signalled the government's intention to increase further the number of Bills receiving pre-legislative scrutiny, stating that 'my view, and more importantly the government's view, is that a Bill should be published in draft form unless there are good reasons for not doing so'.[7]

But before the use of pre-legislative scrutiny becomes more widespread, there are a number of problems that need to be tackled. Most fundamentally, as has been outlined, the government maintains key control over pre-legislative scrutiny. It decides which Bills will be published in draft and whether parliamentary committees will have time to scrutinise them. For example, the Work and Pensions Committee's request to examine the Pensions Bill in draft was declined by the government on the grounds that it wanted to proceed immediately with a formal Bill.[8] The formation of a Business Committee in the Commons, which would seek to organise parliamentary and legislative business on a more consensual basis, could provide a mechanism for greater discussion about which Bills would be candidates for pre-legislative scrutiny.

Another limitation of pre-legislative scrutiny is that generally committees are able to consider solely the outline of proposed legislation and the framework of the powers and provisions contained within it. However, the real impact of a piece of legislation is sometimes contained in its detail, which is introduced after enactment in the form of regulations in delegated (or secondary) legislation. The accompanying regulations are not usually ready when the draft Bill is published and, as a result, pre-legislative scrutiny committees can miss out on the real substance of the Bill. The Joint Committee on the draft Civil Contingencies Bill recommended, 'that in future all enabling Bills published in draft should be accompanied by a comprehensive set of draft secondary legislation'.[9]

Furthermore, the government should drop its opposition to the proposal to allow members of pre-legislative scrutiny committees to speak in subsequent standing committees (but be barred from voting), as suggested by both the Liaison Committee and in a report by the Constitution Unit.[10] That report also recommended that pre-legislative scrutiny committees should provide a 'handbook' for standing committees to enable significant issues to be highlighted. The report noted that no specific body had overall responsibility for pre-legislative scrutiny and proposed that the Liaison Committee, or a designated pre-legislative steering committee, should take responsibility.

Problems with the legislative timetable: There are also practical difficulties with the timetable for drafting and the presentation of draft Bills. The Modernisation Committee drew attention to the fact that draft Bills tend to be published towards the end of the session.[11] As a result, the timescale allocated for pre-legislative scrutiny is frequently inadequate. The Committee hoped that it would be possible for work on draft Bills to continue in parallel with work on Bills which have already been introduced, with the result that pre-legislative scrutiny can take place throughout the session and not just towards its close. The Committee also recommended that where it is not possible to produce a complete legal text the government should submit proposals for pre-legislative scrutiny on the basis of a detailed statement of policy.

The introduction of carry-over of Bills from one parliamentary session to the next could help to mitigate the problems of a constrained timetable. One of the main reasons given for introducing carry-over was to allow greater time for scrutiny of Bills, including pre-legislative scrutiny. Its increased use might allow pre-legislative scrutiny to become a more routine part of the legislative process. As the previous chapter discussed, one notable innovation in recent years has been the introduction of programming of legislation. It has been argued that the advent of programming, and the consequent greater certainty for the government of getting its legislation through, places an obligation on the government to allow better scrutiny and provide clearer explanation of its measures. One obvious way to meet this obligation would be for the government to commit itself to pre-legislative scrutiny for all Bills (with the exception of emergency Bills and other specified cases).

Overloading the select committees: Another concern is that increased pre-legislative scrutiny by select committees might reduce the time available for their oversight and scrutiny functions. At present there seems little evidence that this has become a major problem; some committees have not undertaken pre-legislative scrutiny at all or have undertaken just one inquiry in a session. However, if pre-legislative scrutiny were to be extended to cover all, or almost all, Bills – a reform that many, including the Hansard Society, would wish to see – there might be a danger that their crucial accountability functions might be neglected. To address that potential difficulty, the size of committees could be increased to allow the work to be shared more widely, or sub-committees could be formed either on a standing basis or temporarily to consider particular draft Bills.[12] Furthermore, to respond to changes in government and the development of 'cross-cutting' initiatives and Bills, there should be greater use of joint select committee inquiries or committees of both Houses to reflect the different interests involved.

Conclusion: The Hansard Society welcomes the increased use of pre-legislative scrutiny and supports the extension of its use. The fundamental question is whether pre-legislative scrutiny has improved the quality of legislation. It is impossible to give a definitive answer, as there are no agreed criteria by which to judge and it is also clear that pre-legislative scrutiny is still at a relatively early stage of development, a point underlined by Blackburn and Kennon, who assert that,

'Pre-legislative scrutiny is still experimental and lacks structure. Further development depends more on Government than on Parliament, and on the ability of the cabinet and the "business managers" to decide in advance their future legislative programme, on a department's ability to give drafting instructions, and in particular on the limited resources of the Parliamentary Counsel.'[13]

However, all indications would suggest that it has already been an extremely positive development. The adoption of some further recommendations would help to improve its operation. Most particularly, the government should continue to work towards producing all Bills in draft form (unless exceptional circumstances apply) to allow for pre-legislative scrutiny. Moreover, there should be an aim to have some continuity of membership between committees that examine draft Bills and the standing committees that subsequently examine the formal Bill. Parliament should also continue to experiment with different methods of pre-legislative scrutiny, and should commission research to evaluate and monitor their effectiveness.

Such proposals, would, if implemented, strengthen a feature that is one of Parliament's success stories in recent years. In the case of pre-legislative scrutiny, both Parliament and government have shown that it is possible to make the necessary reforms to improve the way that they do business.

Endnotes and references:

1 *Making the Law: The Report of the Hansard Society Commission on the Legislative Process,* London: Hansard Society (1992).
2 Modernisation Committee (1997-98) *The Legislative Process,* HC 190.
3 The breakdown of the total shows: 1997-98, two Bills; 1998-99, six Bills; 1999-2000, six Bills; 2000-01, two Bills; 2001-02, six Bills; 2002-03, ten Bills; 2003-04, ten Bills.
4 Constitutional Affairs Committee (2003-4) *Judicial Appointments and a Supreme Court (Court of Final Appeal),* HC 48.
5 *Strengthening Parliament: The Report of the Commission to Strengthen Parliament,* chaired by Lord Norton of Louth, Conservative Party: London (2000).
6 Modernisation Committee (2001-2002) *Modernisation of the House of Commons: A Reform Programme,* HC 1168-I.
7 Phil Woolas MP, HC Deb, 24/2/04, vol 418 col 19, WH.
8 See Riddell P. 'Playing Ball and Raising The Game', *The House Magazine,* 10 May 2004.
9 (2002-03) HL Paper 183 and HC 1074 para 226.
10 Power G. *Parliamentary Scrutiny of Draft Legislation: 1997–1999* The Constitution Unit: University College London (2000).
11 Modernisation Committee (2001-2002) *Modernisation of the House of Commons: A Reform Programme.* HC 1168 - I.
12 See *The Challenge for Parliament; Making Government Accountable,* Hansard Society Commission on Parliamentary Scrutiny, chaired by Lord Newton of Braintree (2001) which recommended that there should be an assumption that all backbench MPs should sit on a select committee and that enlarged committees should work through sub-committees.
13 Blackburn R. and Kennon A. *Parliament: Functions, Practice and Procedures* London: Sweet and Maxwell (2003).

5 | Delegated Legislation: Below the Radar

Alex Brazier

Introduction: This chapter looks at delegated (or secondary) legislation, which is law made by ministers under powers in Acts of Parliament (primary legislation). Delegated legislation can be used to amend, update or enforce existing primary legislation without Parliament having to pass a new Act. Regarded by some as a 'tedious corner of the constitutional edifice',[1] the 3,000 or so statutory instruments (SIs) that reach the statute book every year may, at first glance, indeed appear boring and trivial. However, their collective force impacts, as Edward Page notes, on all aspects of daily life: the alarm that wakes us up, the bread we eat for breakfast, the car we drive to work, the roads on which we travel, the content of the tea we drink, even the bed where we sleep.[2] *Making the Law* stressed its importance within the overall legislative process,

'The main advantages of making greater use of delegated legislation outweigh the very real disadvantages…[it] makes Acts easier for the user to follow, helps Parliament to focus on the essential points … [and keeps] the legislative process flexible so that statute law can be kept as up to date as possible … [and eases] pressure on the parliamentary timetable.'[3]

The use of delegated legislation has increased significantly in recent decades; for example, in 1970, SIs filled 4,880 pages of legislation; by 1996 that had grown to 10,230 pages.[4] Yet, despite its volume and importance, its scrutiny by Parliament is widely regarded as inadequate and there have been numerous, but generally unheeded, calls for reform. Primary legislation must go through an elaborate parliamentary process before it becomes law. Although far from perfect, this process provides MPs and Peers with the opportunity to scrutinise and authorise legislation - functions which are crucial to the operation of the democratic system. By contrast, the majority of SIs, with all the powers and controls that they confer, is subject to little, if any, parliamentary scrutiny. This chapter looks at how Parliament scrutinises delegated legislation and at proposals to reform the system.

Parliamentary procedures applying to statutory instruments: SIs can be categorised according to the different degrees of parliamentary scrutiny to which they are subject:

- those that have only to be made, or laid before Parliament, to come into effect;

- those subject to the negative procedure which come into force unless a motion to annul them (known as a prayer) is passed within 40 sitting days;[5]

- those subject to affirmative procedure, which means that they cannot become law unless both Houses first approve a draft;[6]

- so-called 'super-affirmative' instruments which, usually, have to be preceded by 'proposals', which are subject to consultation.[7]

Additionally, the Joint Committee on Statutory Instruments (JCSI), a committee of both Houses, ensures that SIs are made within the powers delegated by the parent Act. It also ensures that the drafting used is not defective and that SIs do not impose a charge on public revenues. However, the JCSI cannot consider the merits of an SI.

Delegated legislation and the House of Lords: An SI cannot be amended by either House and must either be accepted or rejected as it stands. Therefore, the Lords would have to reject an SI entirely if they identified a problem, a path that they are usually unwilling to take. This is despite the fact that the power to reject delegated legislation is one of the few unilateral powers possessed by the Lords (on which they cannot be overruled by the Commons).

The House of Lords has, however, put in place some important mechanisms to strengthen its scrutiny of SIs. It has established a Select Committee on Delegated Powers and Regulatory Reform, which reports on the extent to which powers proposed to be delegated to ministers in Bills appear to be appropriate in particular cases. In 2003, the Lords established the Select Committee on the Merits of Statutory Instruments, which is charged with 'sifting' SIs to determine whether they are of sufficient importance to merit debate. This welcome development to improve scrutiny of delegated legislation is discussed at greater length later in this chapter.

Problems with the system: Given the importance of delegated legislation in the law and governance of the country, the procedures that exist for scrutinising it are almost universally regarded as inadequate. Most criticism is directed at the negative resolution procedure. Under this procedure the initiative lies with the opposition to table appropriate annulment motions in the form of Early Day Motions (known as 'prayers'). However, as the government controls almost all the available parliamentary time in the Commons, unless the opposition can persuade the government to provide time, the SI will not be debated. As the Procedure Committee noted in 2000,

'The reduction in the overall number of negatives debated, at a time when there has been no decrease in the numbers laid or it may confidently be assumed in the complexity or importance of the instruments themselves, strengthens the supposition that existing arrangements for triggering debate on negatives are less than adequate.'[8]

Strengthening Parliament, the Conservative Party Commission report, was even more blunt, stating that the negative resolution procedure 'is close to preposterous. Major changes are needed to existing arrangements.'[9] The Commons Liaison Committee concurred, declaring that the scrutiny of delegated legislation generally was 'woefully inadequate'.[10] In addition to the highly restrictive nature of the scrutiny procedures, a range of specific problems with the passage of SIs has been identified. Among them are concerns that:

- SIs are increasingly being used to implement core policy decisions rather than fill out the detail of statutes;

- an SI can be published after it has come into force, or may also be scheduled to come into force before the time allotted for scrutiny has run its course;

- SIs cannot be amended in part or redrafted;

- the length, volume and technical complexity of many SIs can obscure important issues;

- the implications of an SI for other domestic or EU legislation may not be immediately apparent.

Strong backing for reform: Given the range of criticisms levelled at scrutiny of delegated legislation, it is not surprising that a variety of different proposals have been put forward to improve its operation. *Making the Law* made several recommendations, including that departmental select committees should review SIs in their field prior to their being laid before Parliament and should then report on matters of particular public importance. It also recommended that once an SI had been selected for debate, a Special Standing Committee should undertake more detailed scrutiny, and furthermore, that a Legislation Steering Committee should be set up to determine which prayers should be debated. A steering committee of this sort, the report argued, would standardise the procedure and wrest the allocation of such debates from the control of the government's business managers. Furthermore, the report suggested that rather than merely concentrating on technical details, committees scrutinising SIs should be allowed to question ministers on the purpose, meaning, and effect of the SI. The debate on the SI in the standing committee should be held on the substantive motion approving, rejecting, or otherwise expressing opinions on the SI.

Procedure Committee Reports 1996 and 2000: Although *Making the Law* was able to cite widespread support for its proposals, no significant changes ensued. As a result, demands for reform were repeated, most notably by the Commons Procedure Committee, which produced two broadly similar reports, in 1996 and 2000.[11] One central proposal was the introduction of a 'sifting' committee in both Houses to consider the political and legal significance of individual SIs. The Procedure Committee envisaged that these committees should have the power to call for further information from government departments where necessary. Crucially, they would be able to recommend which negative procedure SIs ought to be debated (regardless of whether any member of either House had prayed against them) and which affirmative SIs could be agreed to without debate (unless six members demanded one).

The Procedure Committee also pointed out that all affirmative resolution SIs are currently debated either in a standing committee or on the floor of the House, though many are of no political interest and are entirely uncontroversial, and the meeting may only last for a few minutes. In contrast, many substantial negative resolution SIs are not subject to any parliamentary scrutiny when, on the face of it, they raise significant issues of which few members of either House are aware. The report proposed the wider use of the 'super-affirmative' procedure to deal with complex SIs in draft, the extension in praying time (during which time opposition parties can call for a debate of the measures) from 40 to 60 days and that neither House should vote on an SI until the JCSI has reported on it.

So far there has been little progress on these recommendations, despite the fact, as the Procedure Committee's report in 2000 noted, that the proposals had been endorsed by the Procedure Committee under both a Conservative and Labour administration, as well as by the Royal Commission on House of Lords Reform and by the Chairmen's Panel in the House of Commons.

Alternative approaches: *Strengthening Parliament* raised the possibility of conditional amendments to SIs whereby an SI could be rejected but the terms under which it would be acceptable would be indicated.[12] The Commission described this as an 'eminently sensible' solution and strongly believed that this represented the best way to proceed. Alternatively, external consultation procedures could be formalised for certain categories of delegated legislation. This model already exists in the field of social security. At present, most draft social security delegated legislation is referred by the government to the Social Security Advisory Committee (SSAC) before being presented to Parliament. The SSAC consults with the public and interested bodies and subsequently produces a report on the likely effects of the SI. The Secretary of State is obliged to take account of the SSAC's recommendations (although is not bound by them) and when the regulations in question are laid before Parliament, the SSAC's report and a statement explaining government responses to the recommendations must also be laid. This model of consultation may be appropriate in other specific areas of legislation.

One important reform implemented: Standing out from the overall pattern of unimplemented proposals, is one recent, significant reform to delegated legislation procedure in the House of Lords. As indicated earlier, this has involved the establishment of a sifting committee to identify SIs 'which it considers to be of sufficient political importance...to merit debate'. The Merits of Statutory Instruments Committee was appointed in December 2003 to serve as a sifting mechanism to identify those SIs that were important and merited further debate or consideration. It considers every SI laid before Parliament and determines whether special attention should be drawn to them. Attention is given on the following grounds:

- that it is politically or legally important or gives rise to issues of public policy likely to be of interest to the House;

- that it is inappropriate in view of the changed circumstance since the passage of the parent Act;

- that it inappropriately implements European Union legislation;

- that it imperfectly achieves its policy objectives.

To date, the Committee has produced numerous reports advising the House on how to scrutinise delegated legislation and has covered issues ranging from scrutiny of draft regional assembly and local government referendums, to horse passports and medicines for human use regulations. Following the decision of the House of Lords to establish the Merits Committee, the Commons' Procedure Committee issued a further report in 2003, which concluded,

'We welcome the Lords' decision to appoint a sifting committee, but emphasise our view that it would be advantageous for discussions to begin immediately with a view to establishing a Joint Committee for sifting delegated legislation from the outset. The alternative of waiting for the Lords' Committee to start and then attempting to join in later strikes us as much less sensible.'[13]

The government rejected the Committee's proposals, claiming that, 'a sifting committee may lead to greatly increased demands on parliamentary time'. The Procedure Committee expressed its disappointment at the government's decision.[14] It is possible that the Lords Merits Committee may, in fact, help the Commons to identify important SIs in the absence of its own sifting committee. However, since the decision to debate SIs subject to the negative procedure lies with the government, any debate would still require its agreement.

Conclusion: Despite its importance, delegated legislation tends to operate below the public and parliamentary radar. It does not have a high priority within Parliament and receives virtually no attention outside it. It is perhaps not surprising, therefore, that in the decade since *Making the Law* noted that 'few, if any, people are satisfied with the attention the Commons pays to delegated legislation', little has changed, in the Commons at least, to challenge that conclusion. On the other hand, the Lords has made significant progress with the establishment of the Merits Committee.

A wide range of bodies has reported on this subject in the last 10 years and all have proposed substantial reforms. The Law Society has identified delegated legislation as a subject for particular consideration as part of its Better Law

Making Programme. Additionally, it is significant that the *Parliament First* group, representing senior MPs of all parties, argued in 2003 that,

'Changes to the way Parliament deals with secondary legislation should be brought forward as a matter of urgency. More detail should be provided within primary legislation and more care taken to provide the best possible legislation through the normal routes.'[15]

While *Making the Law* acknowledged that the increasing use of delegated legislation over recent decades was inevitable, and indeed necessary, given the complexity of modern government and the constraints on parliamentary time, it warned that the mechanisms for achieving effective parliamentary scrutiny were absent. Yet, despite a welter of proposals for reform, the system for scrutinising delegated legislation is exhibiting the same deficiencies identified more than 10 years ago, but in the context of an increasing volume of SIs.

Endnotes and references:

1   See Hayhurst J.D. and Wallington P. 'The Parliamentary Scrutiny of Delegated Legislation' (1998) in Zander M. *The Law Making Process,* London: Butterworth (1994) p.95.
2   Page E.C. *Governing by Numbers:* Delegated Legislation and Everyday Policy-Making Portland: Hart Publishing (2001).
3   *Making the Law: The Report of the Hansard Society Commission on the Legislative Process*, London: Hansard Society (1992).
4   See Procedure Committee (1999-2000) *Delegated Legislation,* HC 48.
5   Most SIs are subject to this 'negative procedure', which means they will become law in the form determined by the minister unless one or other House of Parliament votes against them, and this very rarely happens. The main disadvantage of the negative procedure in the Commons is that there is no requirement for prayers to be debated at all; the decision whether to do so is made by the government.
6   The affirmative procedure, however, is much less common than the negative procedure. For example, in 1998/9, 178 SIs were subject to the affirmative procedure, compared to 1266 subject to negative procedures. See Blackburn R. and Kennon A. *Parliament: Functions, Practice and Procedures* London: Sweet and Maxwell. (2003)
7   This procedure allows for amendments to be proposed by parliamentary committees or others, which the minister may incorporate in the draft order.
8   Procedure Committee (1999-2000) *Delegated Legislation* HC 48.
9   The Commission to Strengthen Parliament, *Strengthening Parliament* (2000) London: Conservative Party.
10   Liaison Committee (1999-2000) *Shifting the Balance: Select Committees and the Executive,* HC 300.
11   Procedure Committee (1995-1996) *Delegated Legislation,* HC 152 and Procedure Committee (1999-2000) *Delegated Legislation,* HC 48.
12   *Strengthening Parliament: The Report of the Commission to Strengthen Parliament,* chaired by Lord Norton of Louth, Conservative Party: London (2000).
13   Procedure Committee (2002-2003) *Delegated Legislation: Proposals for a Sifting Committee,* HC 50.
14   Second Report of the Procedure Committee (2002-2003) *Delegated Legislation: Proposals for a Sifting Committee, the Government's Response to the Committee's First Report,* HC 684.
15   Parliament First, *Parliament's Last Chance* (2003).

6 | Private Members' Bills: Limited Freedom

Alex Brazier

Introduction: Private Members' Bills (PMBs) give backbench MPs and Peers the ability to introduce legislation of their own choosing. In the Commons the system of PMBs began in its current form in the late 1940s and enshrined the notion that a certain amount of parliamentary time should be made available for legislation introduced by individual MPs. The 13 days each year, currently Fridays, formally set aside for PMBs signify a commitment to provide some freedom from the normal constraints that 'government business shall have precedence at every sitting'.[1] However, in the view of many commentators, PMBs have ceased to fulfil the purpose for which they were intended. Yet, despite criticisms of the way that Parliament deals with PMBs, and despite the various legislative reforms since 1997, there have been no significant changes to the procedures governing PMBs in recent years.[2]

How Private Members' Bills become law: A PMB can be introduced by a member of either House who is not a minister. In the Commons, the most effective route is through the ballot held early in each session, which selects 20 Members to have first claim on the time available. PMBs have to negotiate a number of complicated procedural stages if they are to stand a chance of becoming law. For example, on many Fridays, debate on the first Bill will take nearly the whole of the sitting, so that not even all the 20 ballot Bills have the chance to be debated. An MP who is placed lower than seventh in the ballot will have to put the Bill down for Second Reading on a Friday on which it will not be the first to be debated. Otherwise, the MP may hope to have the Bill given a Second Reading without debate at 2.30 pm. With this option, however, if a single Member shouts 'object', the Bill does not receive a Second Reading - even if no other Members are opposed.

Bills also have to secure the Closure, which requires the support of at least 100 MPs. This requirement can be difficult to meet, especially on Fridays when many MPs have constituency business and are therefore away from Westminster. Opponents of a Bill can test the quorum of the House, which requires more than 35 MPs to be recorded as voting; if fewer MPs vote, the House moves immediately on to the next Bill. At Report Stage, small numbers of opponents can table a series of amendments designed to take up time and, ultimately, block a Bill's passage. The 13th Friday allotted for PMBs – colloquially known as 'the slaughter of the innocents' on account of its high attrition rate – is largely taken up with Lords' amendments. By this point, tactical manoeuvres and a complex order of procedural precedence can be used to push a Bill into legislative oblivion.[3]

Finally, once a PMB has passed through the Commons, it must be taken up by a Peer and pass through all stages in the House of Lords. In the House of Lords, Peers have an unrestricted right to introduce PMBs. Bills which have completed all their stages in the Lords are sent to the Commons where they must be taken up by an MP. They are then treated as any other PMB and must pass all the normal stages. Lords Bills often fail to find time to be considered in the Commons as they arrive late in the session and, partly as a result, Lords PMBs rarely become law.

Table 1 shows that the success rate for PMBs (in the Commons) is far below that achieved by government Bills.

Table 1: Success rates of government and Private Members' Bills (%)

Session	Government Bills	Private Members' Bills
1987-88	100.0	10.9
1988-89	100.0	6.3
1989-90	94.4	9.2
1990-91	94.2	16.0
1991-92	86.8	22.0
1992-93	100.0	10.5
1993-94	100.0	13.8
1994-95	94.9	14.5
1995-96	97.7	16.5
1996-97	100.0	26.2
1997-98	98.1	6.7
1998-99	87.1	7.7
1999-00	97.5	5.8
2000-01	60.8	0.0
2001-02	100.0	7.0
2002-03	91.6	13.4

Source: House of Commons Sessional Digests.

Government influence and control: At the time of the 1960s Labour Government, PMBs were used (with the government's active co-operation) to enact legislation that has since had a profound and lasting impact on British society.[4] The reluctance of governments (of both parties) in the past 30 years to provide significant extra time in the parliamentary timetable means that it is unlikely that a succession of such important Bills could now be passed in this way. The more common approach to such 'conscience questions' is for these matters to be introduced in government Bills and for MPs to be given a free vote. In general terms, the government's attitude is the major determining factor in the success of an individual PMB. Few PMBs with any controversial element now pass into law, mainly because the government rarely provides any extra time. Furthermore, the government has in recent years used PMBs as a means of getting 'handout Bills' onto the statute book. Handout Bills involve technical changes to existing laws that the government may not have time to introduce; it therefore seeks a willing MP to take through a Bill on its behalf. Because such Bills come with government support, and because the whips will allow them through their various stages without objecting, they stand a good chance of becoming law. A significant proportion of PMBs could now be categorised as handout Bills; for example, in 1998-99, 11 out of the 20 presented through the ballot were reckoned to be in this category.[5]

As Table 1 showed, the vast majority of PMBs are destined never to reach the statute book. Nonetheless, individual PMBs can have a marked impact even if, ultimately, they do not become law. For example, sometimes a PMB's sponsor will know that the Bill has no chance of becoming law but will proceed solely to attract publicity for a proposed change in the law. Furthermore PMBs can be a way to ensure that the government reveals its intentions in a specific area and ministers sometimes promise to bring in legislation to avoid the passage of a Bill with which they are not content. For example, a succession of PMBs on rights for disabled people from 1992 onwards eventually led to the government passing the Disability Discrimination Act 1995.

Uncertainty and complexity: Even those MPs placed towards the top of the ballot will have no certainty that their Bill will be able to complete all the necessary stages within the prescribed time, even if it has overwhelming majority support. According to Marsh and Read, the PMB process and the loss of Bills which have achieved clear majorities at Second Reading leads, 'not merely, or mainly, to a dissatisfaction with the Private Members' Bills procedure, which few understood, but to a more general disillusionment with Parliament, and the legislative process'.[6]

Furthermore, the PMB system at present is remarkably complex and, in the words of Marsh and Read, 'would baffle an intelligent alien'.[7] Even informed commentators, and MPs themselves, find the procedures arcane in the extreme. A considerable amount of parliamentary time and effort is put into PMBs each year, wasting valuable resources that could be more effectively used. The following example shows how a well-supported PMB can come close to being defeated by a single determined MP. Although it eventually became law, it did so only because of strong government support - a privilege not afforded to the majority of PMBs.

Private Hire Vehicles (London) Bill 1997-98: The proceedings of the Private Hire Vehicles (London) Bill 1997-98 are a good example of the merits and defects of the current PMB system. It shows how a PMB can be a useful tool in introducing important legislation but also demonstrates how a Bill that has strong cross-party support can nevertheless be scuttled by just one MP. It also highlights the crucial importance of government support. Drawn fourth in the ballot, Sir George Young MP introduced, with the support of the three main parties, a PMB that sought to license London's mini-cab trade which, unlike London's black cab trade, had no regulation at all. The Bill obtained a Second Reading and the necessary resolutions needed by 16 March 1998 and the Committee Stage was scheduled for 20 March. However, by objecting on three successive Private Members' Fridays, an MP was able to block the Bill's progress into committee to the point where it was due to be considered on the last available Friday. It was feared that the Bill would be lost in the 'slaughter' that occurs on this day, so the government agreed to allocate the Bill to a standing committee. It then passed all stages and received Royal Assent in July 1998.

Proposals for Reform: The principal benchmark of the PMB process should be the ability to command a majority in both Houses. But an improved success rate for PMBs will not occur without some form of fundamental reform. For this to happen, government as well as Parliament must consent to change. As it stands, it is frequently government whips who object to PMBs to prevent them from making further progress. It is inevitable, and understandable, that the government will wish to stop PMBs to which it is fundamentally opposed. It will not wish to allow its mandated programme to be derailed, be forced to implement measures with which it disagrees or allow the passage of an Act that commits financial resources. These are legitimate concerns and safeguards should be put in place that recognise this reality. Nonetheless, there are ways that the current PMB process could be reformed without undermining the government's legitimate mandate and position, including:

- the introduction of carry-over motions for certain well-supported Bills to prevent them being lost at the end of the session;

- greater use of draft Bills to allow for some form of pre-legislative scrutiny;

- taking Report Stage in standing committees so that the 13 PMB Fridays are used entirely for Second and Third Readings;[8]

- changing the timing of the ballot to the spillover period in October to allow more time for drafting and pre-legislative scrutiny;

- giving select committees a role in putting forward legislation;[9]

- since the change to the Commons' sitting hours in January 2003 extra time exists on Tuesday and Wednesday evenings, which could be allocated to PMBs. The existing Fridays could remain for uncontroversial Bills. These often take up very little time and there is usually no need for many MPs to attend the proceedings. A specific number of evenings could be allocated to more complex but timetabled Bills and extra time could be granted to prevent logjams at the end of a session.

A timetabled approach: The above changes could be relatively easily incorporated into the current PMB system. However, the procedural hurdles that make PMBs so easy to destroy would remain in place. As a result, tactics rather than the merits or level of support, can determine a Bill's fate. The most obvious way to alter that situation, is to devise mechanisms to allow certain Bills to be timetabled and therefore have a greater likelihood of passing through all stages (if both Houses consent). It should be the ability to secure a majority, not the ability to be so inoffensive as to attract no opposition, that should be the hurdle that a PMB should have to surmount.

One method to provide a PMB with a timetabled passage would be through a specific Private Members' Bill Select Committee. A PMB Select Committee could be constituted in a number of ways; possibly by nomination of the whole House or by appointment by the Liaison Committee. If the Committee decided – through unanimous or overwhelming vote – that a PMB had merit, it should have the power to present the Bill for timetabling. The requirement to have all-party support would ensure that the interests of the governing party, and indeed other parties, could not be abused and that only Bills which commanded wide support could make use of a timetabled passage. If a Business Committee were established to formalise the organisation of parliamentary business including the legislative programme, such a body could have a role in moving PMBs towards a timetabled passage.[10]

Andrew Dismore MP proposed that a new select committee should be established to look at a PMB's purpose and provide the government with an opportunity to express its reservations. The committee could then make recommendations using a 'traffic light system':

- Green: it is a sensible Bill, one that meets the committee's agreed criteria, and should proceed, unaltered, with a timetable;

- Yellow: the Bill in principle is fine but needs some extra work. The committee should suggest amendments and, if agreed by the MP in charge, the Bill should be given a timetable. If not, the Bill should proceed as now;

- Red: the Bill does not meet the criteria. The committee would recommend dropping the Bill. The promoter could bring forward a new Bill or proceed with the original Bill under existing procedures without a timetable.

A different method to test support for a Bill and smooth its passage would be to introduce certain thresholds at Second Reading. Procedures could be introduced that moved a Bill towards a timetabled passage if it received clear backing at Second Reading. However, if a certain number of votes were cast against the Bill (say, 40 votes reflecting party balance or 80 votes without party balance) this would prevent the Bill from being timetabled. As the Procedure Committee noted in its 1995 Report, 'it is a matter of debate whether a majority in the House, not supported by an electoral mandate, should be allowed to overcome serious objections from a minority of Members on one issue'.[11]

Alternative PMB procedures: This chapter has so far considered PMBs selected through the ballot but there are other distinct types of PMBs, known as Ten Minute Rule Bills (TMRBs) and Presentation Bills.[12] A considerable amount of both parliamentary and government time is expended on these types of PMBs which have even less chance of becoming law that the ballot Bills. Both TMRBs and Presentation Bills are, in reality, used mainly as a means of attracting publicity and raising awareness of an issue. Reforms might recognise this fact rather than continue with the fiction that the procedures are there primarily for legislative purposes. The time for TMRBs could be used to allow MPs to make short speeches advocating a law change, allow votes on Early Day Motions or consideration of petitions. Additionally, Presentation Bills could be replaced by allowing each MP to publish one draft Bill a year at public expense.

Conclusion: In theory, the PMB procedures that currently exist allow parliamentarians to express themselves in a legislative capacity, regardless of which party is in government. But relatively few PMBs succeed in practice, especially if the minor, technical and handout Bills are taken out of the equation, because they are too dependent on government support and are too easy to destroy. PMB procedures should be made much more straightforward and open, something that the Scottish Parliament has successfully sought to achieve.[13] It is important that if the government, or some other party, wishes to oppose a Bill there should be an assumption that the reasons for this position must be stated openly rather than hidden behind procedural subterfuge.

A reformed PMB system should embody certain principles. These should be that a limited number of well-supported Bills should be able to pass through Parliament without the need for active government support. Bills should not be able to be hijacked by minority opponents but should allow legitimate objection by a significant minority to be raised and prevent passage. Party political manipulation should be avoided and mechanisms, such as voting thresholds or a committee filter, should be established to ensure that this happens. A reformed PMB system could, if properly designed and implemented, enhance the role of backbench MPs and Peers, by enabling them to respond to the concerns of the public.

Endnotes and references:

1 Standing Order 14.

2 Some very minor reforms to the PMB system were proposed by the Procedure Committee report, *Procedures for Debates, Private Members Bills and the Powers of the Speaker* (2002-03) HC 333. The Committee proposed that the government should be ready to provide drafting help for a PMB as soon as it receives a Second Reading and that assistance with drafting should be updated to its 1972 grant level. Currently the 10 Members placed highest in the ballot may claim up to £200 in expenses for help in drafting their Bills. This figure was fixed in 1971 and has not since been revised. If it had been uprated for inflation it would now be worth around £1700.

3 The order of precedence includes consideration of Lords' amendments, Third Readings, new Report Stages, adjourned Report Stages, adjourned committee proceedings, Bills appointed to Committees of the Whole House and Second Readings.

4 Such measures included the initial experimental abolition of capital punishment in 1965, the Abortion Act 1967 liberalising the abortion laws and the Divorce Reform Act 1969.

5 Blackburn R. and Kennon A. *Parliament: Functions, Practice and Procedures,* Second Edition, Sweet and Maxwell, (2003) p 544.

6 Marsh D. and Read M. 'British Private Members' Balloted Bills: A Lottery with Few Winners, Small Prizes, but High Administrative Costs', *Essex Papers in Politics and Government,* University of Essex (1985).

7 Marsh D. and Read M. *Private Members' Bills,* Cambridge University Press (1988).

8 Standing Order 92 allows for this.

9 The Public Administration Select Committee introduced and proposed its own PMB on civil service reform, which, at time of writing, was awaiting its Second Reading in the Commons.

10 See Rush M. and Ettinghausen C. *Opening Up the Usual Channels,* Hansard Society, (2002) and *The Challenge for Parliament; Making Government Accountable,* Hansard Society Commission on Parliamentary Scrutiny, chaired by Lord Newton of Braintree (2001).

11 Procedure Committee (1994-95) Fifth Report, *Private Member's Bills,* HC 38, para 16.

12 For further information on Ten Minute Rule Bills and Presentation Bills, and all other procedural matters on the PMB process, see Blackburn R. and Kennon A. *Parliament: Functions, Practice and Procedures,* Second Edition Sweet and Maxwell (2003).

13 For further information on the Scottish Parliament's legislative process, see Barry K. Winetrobe's chapter *Making the Law in Devolved Scotland.*

7 | Making the Law in Devolved Scotland

Barry K. Winetrobe

Introduction: the principles of the Holyrood legislative process: Since 1999, the Scottish Parliament has been making primary legislation for devolved matters in Scotland, and, as such, it is a useful comparator for Westminster to examine. As a 'Westminster model' Parliament, Holyrood's legislative process has its origins in part in Westminster practice, although the aim has always been to provide a way of making law that is both different and better than that in the UK Parliament.

Those who devised the devolution scheme saw law making as a central feature of the new Parliament, though not its sole function, nor one operated as a discrete activity set apart from its other activities. The Consultative Steering Group (CSG), which was set up by the UK government to advise on how the Scottish Parliament should operate, applied to the legislative process its key principles, especially those of 'power-sharing', and 'access and participation'.[1] The aim was to produce a system of law making, which would:

- be less executive-dominated, both in the devising of the process and in its operation or content;

- involve the public in the process, both in the pre-legislative and parliamentary stages;

- provide meaningful opportunities for the Parliament, through its members and committees, to scrutinise and initiate legislative proposals;

- ensure, as far as possible, that 'good' legislation was enacted, in terms of effectiveness and legal validity.

Features such as the multi-functional committee system, and the organisation of business through the Parliamentary Bureau, were designed to be central to the legislative process, and to the operation of the Parliament generally.

This chapter will outline how laws are made in devolved Scotland, concentrating on those aspects which may be relevant to Westminster, rather than those differences which derive from the structural or constitutional nature of the devolved Parliament which are less relevant. Nonetheless, these latter differences need to be described at the outset.

Constitutional features of the devolved law making context: Scottish devolution is founded on a UK statute, the Scotland Act 1998 (the 1998 Act). As such, the Scottish Parliament and the Scottish Executive are both creatures of statute, and can only do what is within their respective powers. This affects the legislative process in two main ways. The Parliament can only legislate on matters within its 'legislative competence' as defined in the 1998 Act, and any purported exercise of its law making powers is subject to various forms of judicial challenge and ministerial intervention.[2] Furthermore, as a statutory body, with only such protections and immunities as are provided in the Act, its proceedings and internal actions, including those when acting in legislative mode, may also be reviewed by the courts.[3] Because of these limitations, several 'compliance' procedures are in place both before and after the formal parliamentary legislative process to ensure that the Parliament does not exceed its powers and act unlawfully.[4]

As the Scottish Parliament is a unicameral body, there is no need for any procedures to cope with disagreements between two law making Houses, as is the case at Westminster. There is, therefore, additional pressure on the Parliament (especially through its committees, and in pre-legislative scrutiny) to 'get its legislation right' without the benefit of a reviewing chamber.[5] It also removes one convenient way of spreading the burden of the legislative programme cycle, as there is no alternative body in which to introduce Bills.

In a more political sense, the Parliament's electoral system, being a form of proportional representation, makes single-party majority government unlikely. The operation of the Executive as either a formal coalition (as has been the practice), informal coalition or minority administration is bound to have an impact on law making, both in the substance of legislation and in the operation of the parliamentary legislative process. Some aspects of the legislative process are prescribed by, or under, the 1998 Act itself and these take priority over any procedural requirements established later by the Parliament itself in Acts of the Scottish Parliament (ASPs), in Standing Orders (SOs), or otherwise. One main example of this is the requirement in section 36 of the 1998 Act for there to be a three-stage legislative process for Bills.

A brief outline of the Holyrood legislative process: Before highlighting some distinctive features of the Parliament's legislative process, the 'standard' procedure for the enactment of the most common type of public Bill, initiated by the Scottish Executive (an Executive Bill), is outlined.

- Though there is no requirement for any pre-legislative process, generally the introduction of an Executive Bill will be preceded by some form of consultation exercise, which may or may not involve a draft Bill or parliamentary scrutiny.[6] A Bill begins its parliamentary process by its introduction by the relevant Minister, along with a number of 'accompanying documents'.

- The Parliamentary Bureau, the Parliament's business committee, then assigns the Bill to the committee into whose remit the subject matter of the Bill falls (the lead committee) for its Stage 1 scrutiny.

- This scrutiny is in two parts. The lead committee (taking into account the views of any other committees examining the Bill) considers the general principles of the Bill, usually by an inquiry which includes evidence from outside bodies and individuals, and reports to the Parliament on whether it recommends that the Parliament agrees to the Bill's general principles.

- Only then is the Bill debated in plenary, when the Parliament decides whether or not to agree to the Bill's general principles. If it does not agree, the Bill falls.

- If it does agree, the Bureau sends the Bill back to a committee (usually the Stage 1 committee) for Stage 2 scrutiny, which involves detailed scrutiny of its provisions, in practice through consideration of any amendments.

- Finally, the Parliament in plenary may consider further amendments at Stage 3, and then decides whether or not the Bill should be passed. If the Parliament rejects the motion that the Bill be passed, it falls. If the Bill is passed, the Presiding Officer sends it for Royal Assent (subject to the statutory periods for ministerial or law officer intervention[7]), the granting of which by the Sovereign turns the Bill into an Act of the Scottish Parliament.

Some innovative features of the Holyrood legislative process: The following sections consider some of the features of the Parliament's legislative process which, not being inextricably linked to the constitutional features noted above, could be adopted or adapted in some way at Westminster:

- **Unified committee system:** This is probably the most visible aspect of the Holyrood Parliament, combining (to use Westminster terminology) both 'select' and 'standing' functions in one committee, along with other functions such as the consideration of relevant subordinate (or delegated) legislation and petitions. The idea is to encourage the development of subject expertise within a committee, as well as a holistic approach to all aspects of a particular public policy area. Some feared that the non-partisan collegiality of a committee would be undermined when considering matters such as Executive Bills, though experience thus far suggests that this has not been an overwhelming problem. Because of the size of the Parliament (129 MSPs) and the number of committees (excluding private Bill and ad hoc committees, there are currently 16, of which eight are subject committees), memberships are small, and there has been frequent turnover.[8] Ministers, in practice, are not committee members, and so when they (or a backbencher who is not a member of that committee) are in charge of a Bill, they can participate in the committee's proceedings and move amendments, but cannot vote. Committees are generally required to meet in public, though there has been some recent discussion about whether too often they meet in private when discussing draft Stage 1 reports on Bills.[9] Because of their unified nature, a major issue for committees is the organisation of their business, especially the balance between legislative and other work, and the uneven distribution of the legislative workload between committees, depending mainly on the Executive's legislative programme.[10]

- **Arrangement of legislative business:** Unlike Westminster, where business is arranged through the executive-dominated 'usual channels', the Scottish Parliament has a business committee, the Parliamentary Bureau. The Bureau arranges the Parliament's business, including the legislative business of committees by allocating Bills and subordinate legislation to the relevant committee(s) and by setting timescales for the completion of particular stages.[11] The Bureau consists of the Presiding Officer, and a representative (in practice, the business manager) of each party with five or more MSPs, or of any group of five or more MSPs who are members of smaller parties or are 'independents'.[12] As Bureau voting is weighted by party strength, an Executive majority is generally guaranteed, which tends to prioritise the allocation of time for Executive legislation. In relation to legislative business, the main problems are those of time for proper parliamentary scrutiny at each stage (in committee and in plenary); adequate gaps between each stage for consideration and reflection; opportunities for meaningful public involvement through formal consultation exercises or otherwise, and the impact of legislative business on the committees' ability to carry out other self-generated activities (such as policy inquiries, including pre-legislative scrutiny).[13] More generally, while it is a more formal and inclusive process than at Westminster, the Bureau system is still a relatively private, non-transparent process, and can be regarded more as an institutionalisation, rather than a replacement, of the 'usual channels' arrangements.

- **The legislative programme:** The Parliament operates on a four-year session, thus removing the problem of uncompleted Bills falling at the end of a Westminster-style 'annual' session. However, in practice, the Executive has tended to operate an annual cycle for its legislative programme (usually beginning in late spring and ending at the summer recess of the following year), perhaps because of familiarity with this annual rhythm, or as a discipline on itself and its backbenchers. Though there is no 'Queen's Speech' as such, standing orders allow the First Minister to make a plenary statement setting out 'the proposed policy objectives and legislative programme of the Scottish Executive for any parliamentary year'.[14] The (post-election) coalition agreements of 1999 and 2003 have set out detailed legislative intentions, operating akin to manifesto commitments in mandate terms, and, despite some hopes of a relatively low level of primary legislation, the legislative pressure has been maintained.[15] This is inevitably due in part to public and media expectations, feeding into the desire of the Parliament and the Executive to be seen to be actively governing on their behalf, and also because the development of non-Executive legislation has not led to any corresponding reduction in Executive Bills.

- **Consultation, public engagement and pre-legislative scrutiny:** The involvement of the public (whether individuals or groups) is an integral element of the Holyrood culture, including the legislative process. The CSG Report proposed a pre-legislative scheme which was Executive-led, but examined by committees for their adequacy and effectiveness. This scheme was not translated into the Parliament's standing orders, and so these matters are primarily ones for the Executive (or, for non-Executive Bills, the relevant MSP or committee) and the Parliament and its committees, to determine in relation to particular Bills, draft Bills or other legislative proposals. This can lead to consultation overload and duplication, and deter meaningful public involvement, especially by those individuals and groups who are not 'the usual suspects'. The introduction of an Executive Bill must be accompanied by a Policy Memorandum outlining what, if any, consultation took place, and a summary of its outcome.[16] There have been criticisms that the Executive has not been meeting its targets of two rounds of consultation and the production of a draft of each major Bill. Public engagement also requires the provision of sufficient and accessible information on legislation and the legislative process. The Parliament seeks to achieve this by, for example, exploiting online techniques; publishing detailed procedural guidance aimed primarily at MSPs and staff (but available online) and by its staff being willing to provide advice.[17]

- **Types of Bills:** Bills are divided into public Bills and private Bills, each with their own procedure set out in Standing Orders. Public Bills can be divided further by their provenance: Executive Bills; Members' Bills, and Committee Bills, the latter two known collectively as Non-Executive Bills. Other than differences relating to their initial proposal and introduction, the formal three-stage legislative process is substantially the same for all these types.[18] The scope for individual MSPs and, especially, committees to initiate primary legislation is fundamental to the Parliament's principle of power-sharing. However, there are inevitable tensions, and competition for time and resources, between Executive and non-Executive legislation, with the Executive naturally regarding its programme as sacrosanct. Unlike the House of Commons, there is no dedicated plenary time for non-Executive Bills. In 2000, the Parliament established a non-Executive Bills Unit (NEBU) to assist MSPs and committees, but there has been great pressure on its limited resources. The Procedures Committee published a major review of Members' Bills in mid-2004, with proposals for improving the process.[19]

- **Accompanying documents:** Other than statements of legislative competence, Bills have to be accompanied by a range of explanatory documents on their introduction, depending on the type of Bill. A standard Executive Bill has to be accompanied by a financial memorandum (setting out 'best estimates of the administrative, compliance and other costs' of the Bill's measures); explanatory notes ('which summarise objectively what each of the provisions of the Bill does…and give other information necessary or expedient to explain the effect of the Bill'), and a policy memorandum (setting out the policy objectives of the Bill; alternative ways considered of meeting these objectives; any consultation undertaken and its outcome, and assessment of the Bill's impact on a range of factors, such as equal opportunities and sustainable development). This material, in terms of its range of content, is clearly of potential value in the legislative scrutiny process, though doubts have been cast on just how much they are being used directly by MSPs, as opposed to the interested wider public and pressure groups, when examining Bills.[20]

- **Post-legislative scrutiny:** This is generally recognised as an important area where Parliaments do not do as good a job as they should, and Holyrood is no exception. The Procedures Committee's 'founding principles' report in 2003 recommended that Standing Orders should at least require committees to consider regularly the need for such scrutiny, and commended the framework produced by the then Social Justice Committee.[21]

- **Subordinate legislation:** Scrutiny of subordinate legislation is an important function of any Parliament. It is fair to say that, thus far, the Scottish Parliament has operated a substantially similar scrutiny system to that which operates at Westminster (with all the associated problems of workload and time pressures), though it may decide to legislate in future to create more distinctive arrangements. The main work is undertaken by the Subordinate Legislation Committee, which undertakes technical examination of instruments in a roughly similar fashion to Westminster's Joint Committee on Statutory Instruments. Perhaps the most distinctive feature of the Holyrood arrangements is that scrutiny of the merits of instruments is undertaken by the committee dealing with the relevant public policy area, rather than by dedicated delegated legislation committees.

Scope for Westminster changes based on Holyrood practice: Though transfer (especially ill-considered 'cherry-picking') of procedure and practice from one Parliament to another is fraught with dangers, it is possible to identify two broad categories of changes derived from Holyrood's legislative process, that Westminster could consider. The first category covers those areas which could be adopted or adapted into the current Westminster arrangements with little difficulty. Examples would be:

- a standard scheme of 'accompanying documents' on the introduction of Bills, requiring them to cover at least the range of issues as are in the Holyrood documents;

- a procedure whereby committees can not only draft proposed legislation, but can also, in some way set out in Standing Orders, seek to ensure that its proposed legislation is subject to a legislative process which can lead to its enactment;[22]

- the creation of a dedicated body akin to the Non-Executive Bills Unit, to assist backbenchers and committees with their legislative proposals;

- publication of detailed procedural guidance on the legislative process that is currently regarded as internal documentation;

- combined committee inquiry/plenary debate consideration of Bills at an early stage, by routine use of select committees or special standing committees (and their Lords equivalent).

The second category covers those aspects which require a more substantial change in Westminster's two Houses, and probably not just directly in their legislative procedures. The main examples would be:

- the adoption and publication of a set of principles for the operation of legislative (and other) business, so that all concerned - including the government, all MPs and the public - know what are the aims and objectives of the legislative process, both generally and in its component parts, and their respective roles in the process;

- a unified committee system in place of separate select, standing committees and other ad hoc legislative committees;

- a full-Parliament legislative cycle in place of the present sessional arrangement;

- some form of business committee, to arrange and allocate all legislative (and other) business.

Conclusion: This broad overview of the Scottish Parliament's legislative process has concentrated on those areas which may be most relevant to the Westminster situation. The legislative process at Holyrood is by no means perfect, with familiar problems of party and Executive-Parliament tensions; media and public criticisms and expectations; and time and resource constraints. It is still too early in the life of the devolved parliament to make any considered assessment of the effectiveness of its legislative process in terms of the 'quality' of its legislative output, however that may be defined.

Nevertheless, the key difference between Holyrood and Westminster is a fundamental one of culture, with the Scottish Parliament seeking to operate, legislatively and otherwise, within its stated key principles. In this way, it aims to involve the public more in the legislative process; to integrate its legislative work with its other functions and activities, and generally to try to make the legislative process as effective and meaningful as possible. Westminster is slowly coming round to these ideas, though the more holistic approach of Holyrood still seems far off.[23] Reform of the Westminster legislative process, if considered and introduced properly, would not just benefit the scrutiny and quality of legislation, but may also be a catalyst for more fundamental reform of the UK Parliament itself.

Endnotes and references:

1   Scottish Office, *Shaping Scotland's Parliament* (1999) especially chapter 5. Much of its philosophy and proposals have been put into practice in the Parliament, though it has been criticised for political naivety (especially its failure to address the centrality of party within a Parliament). The importance of the principles (the others being 'accountability' and 'equal opportunities') lies more in the culture generated by them collectively rather than individually. See generally Winetrobe B. *Realising the vision: a parliament with a purpose*, Constitution Unit (2001) and the Procedures Committee's major review of the operation of the CSG Principles *The founding principles of the Scottish Parliament* (2003) Third Report, March 2003.
2   This also applies to the Executive's 'devolved competence' to make subordinate legislation.
3   The Parliament does not enjoy any Westminster-style inherent parliamentary privilege.
4   The division of legislative power between the two Parliaments has also led to Westminster continuing to legislate for Scotland in some devolved areas with Holyrood's consent, under the so-called 'Sewel Convention'. This is a controversial issue, and not directly relevant to this chapter.

5   In his evidence to the Lords Constitution Committee, the first Presiding Officer, Sir David Steel said: 'I put it this way: we do the revising process first'; *Devolution: inter-institutional relations in the UK* (2002-03) HL147, p754, p205.

6   The internal Executive processes for developing, drafting and prioritising particular legislative proposals, though important in themselves, are outside the scope of this chapter.

7   Such intervention may trigger a further stage, 'reconsideration', where the Bill may be considered and amended by the Parliament, to make it suitable for enactment.

8   On the impact of such features see Arter D. 'On assessing strength and weakness in parliamentary committees: some preliminary observations on the new Scottish Parliament' (2002) 8 *Journal of Legislative Studies* 93.

9   Virtually all committee papers are published on the Parliament's website in advance of committee meetings, which is a major aid to openness and public participation.

10   Early on, the legislative and other workload of the Justice and Home Affairs Committee led to the creation of two justice committees, each with the same remit.

11   Strictly, it *proposes* these arrangements to the Parliament, which then debates and decides on whether to accept them.

12   In the first session, four parties were represented (Labour, SNP, Conservative and Liberal Democrat); in the current session, seven (with the addition of the Greens and Scottish Socialists, and from September 2004, a group of the five independent and single-member-party MSPs).

13   These issues were highlighted in the Procedures Committee's 'founding principles' report, and, at the time of writing (late summer 2004) are being examined in a major inquiry by that Committee.

14   A parliamentary year begins with the first meeting of the Parliament after an election, or with an anniversary of that date (normally, therefore, May-to-May). In practice, these statements have been made each year either in May/June or in September, with a programme designed to be completed by the following summer recess.

15   At least, after an initial burst to clear the perceived logjam of Scottish legislation at Westminster, mainly dealing with technical law reform.

16   In practice, Members' Bills must also go through an adequate form of consultation for them to 'qualify' for assistance from the Parliament's Non-Executive Bills Unit (NEBU).

17   The most relevant example is the *Guidance on Public Bills* (2001) Second Edition but there is also *Guidance on Private Bills,* and for objectors to private Bills, as well as guidance on legislative issues within the general guidance for committees.

18   One difference is that Committee Bills do not have a Stage 1 committee inquiry prior to their plenary debate. Bills can be further classified by content or procedure - Budget Bills, Consolidation Bills, Statute Law Repeals Bills, Statute Law Revision Bills and Emergency Bills.

19   *A new procedure for members' Bills* (July 2004) Sixth Report, session 2. At the time of writing, this important report has not yet been considered by the Parliament in plenary.

20   Mullen T. 'Scottish Parliament legislation 1999-2002' (2003) 9 *European Public Law* 179, at p187.

21   *op cit,* vol 1 paras 371-382. In its response to the report, the Executive was, unsurprisingly, not convinced of the need for a standard framework for such scrutiny.

22   See, for example, the Public Administration Committee's draft Civil Service Bill in its First Report, 2003-04, *A Draft Civil Service Bill: Completing the Reform,* HC 128.

23   See, for example, the Commons Modernisation Committee's report, *Connecting Parliament with the public* (June 2004) First Report, HC 368 and the Lords Constitution Committee Report, *Parliament and the Legislative Process* (2003-04) HL 173.

8 | Law Making for Wales

David Lambert and Marie Navarro

Introduction: The law making process for Wales has changed considerably since the coming into effect of devolution. As stated in the 1997 White Paper, *A Voice for Wales,* 'The government is committed to establishing a new, more inclusive and participatory democracy in Britain. Its proposals for a Welsh Assembly reflect these aims.'[1] It implemented the subsidiarity principle in the United Kingdom, and in Wales, by stating: 'By establishing the Assembly, the government is moving the process of decision-making closer to the citizens: many more decisions about Wales will be made in Wales.'[2] But in the context of Welsh devolution, only secondary legislation has been devolved. Therefore, law making for Wales has been divided in two; Westminster remains the sole maker of primary legislation for Wales and the Welsh Assembly has an important role in secondary legislation. This is in contrast to the devolution settlements for Scotland and Northern Ireland, where both primary and secondary legislation competences have been devolved.

Since July 1999, there has been a National Assembly for Wales (NAW). The Assembly was established under the Government of Wales Act 1998 (GOWA) following a referendum in 1997 held under the Referendums (Scotland and Wales) Act 1997. The referendum was on a government proposal to create an executive body that would have both executive powers and also powers to make subordinate (secondary) legislation but not primary legislation.[3] In the referendum, 50 per cent of those who were eligible to vote in Wales did not do so, and of the remaining 50 per cent, 49.6 per cent voted against the proposal and 50.1 per cent voted in favour: a majority of 6,500.

GOWA provides that the Assembly is a unitary corporate body with 60 Members. All its functions are statutorily vested in the Assembly as a whole, either under the transfer orders made under GOWA, under post-devolution Acts or under designation orders made under section 2(2) of the European Communities Act 1972. The Assembly has the powers exercised by the Secretary of State for Wales under 350 Acts of Parliament. The Assembly has established the practice of delegating all its functions, other than those which it is required by law to exercise itself, to the Assembly First Minister.[4] The law making powers of the Assembly comprise executive and subordinate legislative powers under some 400 Acts of Parliament and orders made under the European Communities Act 1972.

Primary legislation: It was clearly stated from the beginning of the process that 'Parliament will continue to be the principal law maker for Wales'.[5] The United Kingdom Parliament decides what powers, if any, are to be given to the Assembly under primary legislation or designation orders. There are no statutory principles in GOWA, or any other agreed principles, guiding Parliament as to the subject areas for which the Assembly could be made responsible and whether the Assembly has powers depends on the provisions of each particular Act.[6]

Within Acts giving powers to the Assembly, there is no guarantee that all ministerial powers exercisable by central government in England will similarly be exercisable by the Assembly in relation to Wales. In most Acts of this type, powers are also given to central government on a Wales and England basis. Table 1 below shows how many Acts per year give powers to the Assembly[7]:

Table 1: Number of Acts giving powers to the Welsh Assembly

Years	Number of Acts devolving powers to NAW
TFO[8] 1999 (1841-1998)	350
1999	5
2000	14
2001	7
2002	12
2003	13
2004	9

In Acts giving powers to the Assembly, it is unusual, but not impossible, for the Assembly to be given different powers to those given to ministers in relation to England. One example is the Planning and Compensation Act 2004 which gave the Assembly different powers to central government to create a central planning process for Wales.

Section 31 of GOWA requires the Secretary of State for Wales to undertake such consultation with the Assembly, following the annual Queen's Speech to

Parliament, about the government's legislative programme 'as appears to him to be appropriate'. GOWA followed most of the concepts contained in the White Paper; that is, it gave the Secretary of State the key role and responsibility for proposing primary legislation. No formal machinery has been established by which the Assembly as a whole can seek to influence the provisions of Bills in Parliament. No direct intervention of the Assembly is provided for; the Secretary of State for Wales remains the only person to consider the representations about the Assembly's primary legislative needs. Recently, the House of Commons Welsh Affairs Select Committee, and the Assembly, agreed that the select committee and the relevant Assembly subject committee would together scrutinise draft Bills that propose to give powers solely to Wales. However, on average, since 2000 there has only been one such Bill in each parliamentary session.

In relation to England and Wales Bills, the Assembly's standing orders enable its subject committees to consider the provisions of Bills and draft Bills. However, there is no formal liaison between these committees and the committees of either House of Parliament. Therefore, while Assembly government ministers, and their officials, seek to liaise over Bills with the Secretary of State and other central government ministers, the Assembly subject committees have no established mechanisms to transmit their views to Parliament. In any case, by the time the subject committees have considered these Bills, it is usually too late to influence their passage at Westminster.

Recent reports on the legislative process: The legislative situation has been considered in three different reports. In January 2003 the House of Lords Constitution Committee made a number of recommendations to improve Westminster legislation affecting the National Assembly.[9] One recommendation is that both distinct Wales provisions in England and Wales Bills, or Wales-only Bills, should be considered by the Welsh Affairs Select Committee to allow evidence to be taken from interested parties including Assembly members. A further recommendation was that consideration should be given to allow Assembly members the opportunity to consider relevant Bills as they progress through Parliament. This would necessitate taking account of the different ways of working and timescales applying to both the Assembly and the Westminster Parliament.

Also in 2003, the House of Commons Welsh Affairs Select Committee emphasised the need for an effective relationship between Westminster and the

National Assembly for Wales.[10] The committee considered this to be a crucial factor for the success of Welsh devolution and recognised that, at present, there is no machinery for formal joint working between Westminster committees and the Assembly. The report recommended that the Commons Procedure Committee should consider formal joint meetings between Commons select committees and subject committees of the National Assembly. It further considered ways in which the Assembly as a whole, and its members, could make their views known formally at Westminster on legislation that directly affects Wales. For this purpose, the report recommended that consideration should be given to committing a Wales part of a Bill to a separate standing committee and that Special Standing Committee procedures should be used for consideration of any Wales-only Bill. The government's response to the report was non-committal as to whether these recommendations should be adopted.[11]

The latest report, produced by the Richard Commission in 2004, was written by a non-statutory body established by the coalition government of the First Assembly.[12] This report was by far the most critical and its recommendations the furthest reaching. It advised that only the granting of legislative functions to Wales (in certain subject areas) would bring stability to the devolution settlement and to the Welsh system of governance. Its recommendations are considered later in this chapter.

Secondary legislation: The Assembly and central government: In its capacity as a legislator for Wales, the National Assembly for Wales has two main functions. It can make secondary legislation either on its own, together with central government departments or with the devolved Scottish or Northern Irish bodies. It can also approve secondary legislation made by local authorities and other public bodies (including central government) submitted to it for approval.

The Assembly's law making functions reflect the functions of central government ministers. Therefore, it has powers to make both general and local statutory instruments (SIs) and other subordinate legislation such as directions, schemes, codes, rules and general determinations. Its general SI powers include the making of commencement orders to implement provisions of Acts. Consequently, Acts can give powers both to central government, and to the Assembly, to commence provisions of Acts. Thus central government is enabled to commence certain provisions of an Act in relation to England only or in relation to England and Wales. The Assembly is able to commence certain provisions in relation to Wales. Assembly orders and regulations can also implement EU Directives and, additionally, there are limited powers to amend or repeal primary legislation (the so-called Henry VIII powers).

The general approach adopted by Parliament in giving secondary legislative powers to the Assembly, is to allow the Assembly to decide how to put into operation a philosophy, which is common to both England and Wales provided that there are no cross-border issues. Therefore, for example, health matters which are common to England and Wales such as professional qualifications and a central NHS salary structure are matters for central government in both countries. Health matters relating to Wales only are for the Assembly to implement. In the field of health, as Table 2 shows, central government is still highly involved in the making of secondary legislation for Wales.[13]

Table 2: Secondary legislation relating to health made by central government and the National Assembly for Wales

Year	Central Government	NAW
1999	22	5
2000	72	11
2001	31	18
2002	81	26
2003	71	40
2004 (up to 01/06)	27	24

General SIs made by central government for England and Wales continue to be subject to the usual parliamentary scrutiny of negative or affirmative resolution procedures (depending on the particular provision of the enabling Act). Such SIs are not subject to any Assembly procedure of scrutiny or consideration (except in the few cases where the SIs are made jointly, concurrently, after consultation with, or with agreement of either the Assembly or central government). With few exceptions, SIs made by the Assembly are not subject to parliamentary scrutiny. They follow a special Assembly procedure; Parliament is not even involved when the Assembly is given powers to amend primary legislation, although at present such powers are rare.

Assembly scrutiny of subordinate legislation: The Richard Commission considered that 'secondary legislation is one of the most tangible outcomes of the Assembly's work'. This is supported by the number of general SIs which the Assembly makes each year. From 2001, this has averaged over 200, as Table 3 illustrates:[14]

Table 3: General statutory instruments made by the Welsh Assembly 1999-2004

Year	General SIs
1999 (from 05/08)	30
2000	124
2001	242
2002	224
2003	217
2004 (up to 01/11)	233

The Government of Wales Act and the Assembly Standing Orders generally require Assembly subject committees and the Assembly in plenary to scrutinise draft general SIs proposed by the Assembly government. The Assembly decides whether they should be made. In practice, as the Richard Commission has commented, during the first Assembly from July 1999 to April 2003 the Assembly subject committees spent only two per cent of their time scrutinising subordinate legislation. The Assembly in plenary only spent nine per cent of its time in such scrutiny.

While both the subject committees and the Assembly in plenary can move amendments to draft SIs, they moved very few in the first Assembly.[15] The situation may change in the second Assembly as a result of the implementation of the recommendations of the Assembly Review of Procedure Group, which were published in February 2002.[16] This Review recommended that Assembly ministers prepare timetables, to be updated at regular intervals, giving notice to Assembly subject committees of draft SIs which the committees will consider in the coming months. However, in May 2003, it was decided that the committees would only meet every three weeks while the Assembly is in session and then only for three hours.

The nature of Assembly statutory instruments: With few exceptions, GOWA requires that Assembly general SIs shall be in both English and Welsh. This requirement, together with the procedures required for scrutiny and approval of such SIs, usually results in a time-lag between central government making an

SI for England and the Assembly making an SI for Wales under the same powers. Sometimes the time difference can be as much as a year or more, and this, therefore, results in different law being applicable in England, and separately in Wales, in the interim period. Thus, the power in a new Act of Parliament to commence provisions of the Act in relation to England can be exercised some time before the Assembly exercises the equivalent power for Wales.[17] Sometimes an SI is made for England with no equivalent made by the Assembly or vice versa. If the Assembly does make an equivalent, it may be the same or different to that made for England. It is not generally realised that with an average of over 200 general SIs being made by the Assembly each year, as well as other non-SI subordinate legislation, the law in Wales is becoming different in a number of important areas to that of England.

Non-SI subordinate legislation: As regards Assembly subordinate legislation not made by SIs, there is no scrutiny procedure equivalent to that used for Assembly general SIs. Nevertheless, unlike the situation that applies to central government, where non-SI subordinate legislation normally requires no parliamentary consideration, the Welsh devolution scheme provides a potential scrutiny device. This includes consideration by Assembly subject committees (if Assembly ministers so decide) and the Assembly in plenary (if at least 10 Assembly members so decide).[18]

Publication of Assembly subordinate legislation: The Assembly has its own website. However, it is difficult to identify from that the full extent of the subordinate legislation made by the Assembly or its ministers. General SIs made by the Assembly are published on the HMSO website, which has a Wales section setting out the legislation applying primarily or mainly to Wales, including the SIs made by the Assembly. However, there is no such special categorisation for SIs made by central government alone applying both to England and Wales. Local SIs made by the Assembly are not listed on the HMSO website (unless they are published by HMSO), nor is non-SI subordinate legislation made by the Assembly. Furthermore, there is no central or comprehensive list on the Assembly website setting out its non-SI subordinate legislation.

The result is that, for practitioners and other people in Wales, the totality of the current law made by the Assembly, or applying to Wales, is difficult to ascertain.

While this is also a problem in England, the Assembly's Standing Order 30 requires the Assembly to publish any subordinate legislation made or confirmed by it, which is not published by HMSO. This is a provision which is unique to the Welsh devolution settlement.

The Richard Commission: The Richard Commission was appointed in July 2002 by the coalition government of Labour and Liberal Democrats which existed during the last three years of the first Assembly.[19] Its appointment was a requirement of the Liberal Democrats before entering the coalition. The Commission reviewed the adequacy of the Assembly's powers and its electoral arrangements. In its report published in March 2004, the Commission considered that the Assembly government should be able to formulate policies within clearly defined fields and should be able to set its own priorities and timetables for action. To achieve this, the Commission did not think that the present executive power system was a sustainable basis for future long-term development. While accepting that the Assembly's powers had evolved significantly since 1999, the evolution had been ad hoc. It was piecemeal development on a case-by-case basis not based upon any agreed general policy or informed by any clear set of devolution principles. The report observed that,

'The legislative relationship between Cardiff, Whitehall and Westminster has grown significantly, but remains dependent upon particular situations and even individual departmental inclinations… Even with good will on both sides, there are practical constraints on the achievement of the Assembly's legislative requirements.'[20]

With the exception of one Commission member, Mr Ted Rowlands, who considered that it was not the time to recommend an alternative devolution model for Wales, the members recommended the adoption of primary legislative and executive powers by the Assembly in the 18 subject areas listed in Schedule 2 to GOWA. The problems of clearly defining the legislative competencies within the areas were not considered. There is no subject area where the Assembly currently has full executive competency. Central government retains powers in every area in relation to Wales. The Commission did not explain why central government would surrender these powers and agree to recommend to Parliament the granting of full primary legislative and executive functions to the Assembly in the 18 subject areas.

Pending the implementation of such legislation, which would include the formal separation of the Assembly executive from the Assembly as a legislature, the report recommended giving wide general executive powers, including order making powers, to the Assembly to implement the objectives of new Acts of Parliament. With regard to electoral arrangements the report recommended an increase of 20 Members from 60 to 80 and for the replacement of the present electoral system with all Members being elected under the single transferable vote system.[21]

In the face of opposition by a number of Welsh Labour MPs to the report's proposals, the Assembly's First Minister suggested that the interim solution (proposed in the report) to give wide executive powers to the Assembly could be the basis for a new Act (or Acts). These would enable the Assembly (by order) to make such provisions, including the amendment or repeal of any existing Act as the Assembly considers necessary, to achieve the objectives of its policies regarding health (or any of the other subject areas listed in Schedule 2 to GOWA). While this is legislatively unprecedented, (with the possible exception of the Regulatory Reform Act 2001), and has produced concerted criticism from the opposition parties in the Assembly, it nevertheless appears to have gained some support from Welsh Labour MPs.[22]

Many Assembly members, as well as the First Minister and many Welsh MPs, consider it inevitable that a referendum would be required before any future proposals to give the Assembly primary legislative powers could be put to Parliament.

Conclusion: The law making powers for Wales are split in two. The Assembly has control over some of the secondary legislation applying to Wales but has no real capacity to influence the Westminster Parliament in the making of primary legislation for Wales. However, the division of such law making functions, between primary and secondary legislation, is not clear. With regard to subordinate legislation, there are no principles on which the Assembly can build a legitimate expectation as to the powers it will get each year. It is often difficult to ascertain which subordinate legislation made by Whitehall applies to England and Wales. It is also difficult to find out all the legislation that is produced by the NAW. Furthermore, the Assembly has outgrown its present legal structure and change is needed.

As Lord Richard has emphasised, there are fundamental constraints and problems with the current settlement. It is difficult to foresee what changes, if any, will be made to the Assembly's powers and its structure. For the present, the Assembly will continue to derive its powers on an Act-by-Act basis,[23] many of which make it impossible to ascertain whether a power is exercisable in Wales by the Assembly or by central government.[24]

Endnotes and references:

1   Government White Paper, *A Voice for Wales* (1997) Cm3718, para 3.1.
2   *ibid.* para 3.2
3   Set out in *A Voice for Wales.*
4   Under section 62 of the GOWA.
5   *A Voice for Wales* para 3.37.
6   The subject fields set out in Schedule 2 to GOWA only set out the subjects within which the first Transfer of Function Order could give statutory powers to the Assembly.
7   David Lambert and Marie Navarro, *The legislative scope of the Assembly,* presentation for Economic and Social Research Council, June 2004.
8   Transfer of Functions Order - the first Order in Council made under GOWA giving the Assembly its initial powers.
9   *Constitution Committee (2002-03) Devolution: Institutional Relations in the United Kingdom* HL 28.
10 Welsh Affairs Committee (2002-03) Fourth Report *The Primary Legislative Process as it affects Wales,* HC 79.
11 Welsh Affairs Committee (2002-03) *The Government Response to the Fourth Report of the Committee: The Primary Legislative Process as it affects Wales.* HC 989.
12 Published by the Welsh Assembly in March 2004.
13 David Lambert and Marie Navarro, *The legislative scope of the Assembly*, presentation for Economic and Social Research Council, June 2004.
14 *ibid.*
15 Nine were moved during debates in the plenary Assembly and none was successful, see p 62, para 49 of the Richard Commission Report.
16 This was an internal Assembly Group comprising Assembly Members from the four Assembly political parties established in December 2000.
17 This was the case for example with the Commonhold and Leasehold Reform Act 2002.
18 NAW Standing Order 27.
19 In the second Assembly there is now a Labour Government with an overall majority of one.
20 Report by Lord Richard, Welsh Assembly (2004) para 18.
21 Whereby 40 of the 60 Members are elected on a first past the post system and the remaining 20 by the additional members system.
22 For a consideration of this proposal see Alan Trench's article in the summer 2004 edition of *'Agenda'* published by the Institute of Welsh Affairs. The proposal is set out in the Welsh Labour Party document *Better Governance for Wales.*
23 Professor R. Rawlings *Delineating Wales - Constitutional, Legal and Administrative Aspects of National Devolution* (2003) University of Wales, considers this problem in detail in Chapter 9.
24 A recent example is the Anti-Social Behaviour Act 2003 which does not make it clear in its contents or side-headings that Part I contains only central government powers for England and Wales, Part 2 gives powers to the Assembly and the remaining powers are exercisable either by central government or the Assembly in relation to Wales.

9 | The Impact of European Community Law on the British Legislative Process

Paul Double

Introduction: Speaking in the Commons debate in May 1967 before Parliament approved the UK's application to join what was then the European Communities the Prime Minister, Harold Wilson observed,

'It is important to realise that Community law is mainly concerned with industrial and commercial activities, with corporate bodies rather than private individuals. By far the greater part of our domestic law would remain unchanged after entry.'[1]

It is not easy to assess precisely how much domestic law now owes its origins to Europe. A Cabinet Office report in October 2002 estimated that around 50 per cent of 'significant legislation' enacted in the UK originates from the European Union.[2] Whilst such estimates inevitably involve a degree of empiricism, the influence of Europe on UK law making is now an established fact and is far more broad ranging than was anticipated in the parliamentary debates when the decision to join was made.[3]

The impact of Community law: To assess the impact of European Community law (referred to in this chapter as Community law) on the UK legislative process, the way that it relates to domestic legislation needs to be considered. In this regard, the issue of parliamentary supremacy in the face of Community law, and how Parliament maximises its opportunities for influencing European initiatives, are particularly relevant. The domestic legislative process will lose its relevance if it does not influence what actually emerges in the rights and obligations that affect people 'on the ground'.

The European Court of Justice (ECJ) was set up as the ultimate adjudicator of Community law; its perspective of how Community and national laws relate to each other is highly influential. Even before the UK joined the Community in 1973, the Court had demonstrated its willingness to interpret Treaty provisions to further what it saw as the underlying vision of the European project. In the *Van Gend en Loos* case,[4] a Netherlands import duty, which had been increased by domestic legislation, was alleged to contravene a Treaty article that disallowed such increases.[5] The Netherlands, German and Belgian governments submitted observations and, in various ways, made the point that articles of the Treaty should not be taken as conferring rights which individuals could rely on to trump a national law. The ECJ, by applying a principle of its own invention, that of 'direct effect', found that the company could enforce the Treaty article in the Netherlands' courts.

According to the Court, the (European Economic) Community had created a 'new legal order' of international law and the participating states had, in consequence, limited their sovereign rights; 'Community law not only imposes obligations on individuals but is also intended to confer on them rights which become part of their legal heritage'. It is of interest that this 'new legal order' was arrived at by the ECJ even though this was seemingly contrary to what the governments of three member states – half the Community at that time – understood they had signed up to.

The British context: In the British context, the 'new legal order' has therefore been operational since 1 January 1973.[6] The practical consequence – the enforceability of directly effective Treaty articles by individuals – has accordingly been available since then, without further parliamentary sanction. The UK legislative process must take that availability as read; it is not a matter in which Parliament has a discretion. Parliament therefore needs, by necessity, to frame its legislation to be consistent with the Treaty articles that confer individual enforcement rights. Numerous articles have been invested with this characteristic by the ECJ, including those on free movement of persons and goods, on equal pay and competition.[7]

Parliamentary debates at the time of the UK's accession made specific reference to the ability of the EC Treaty to confer rights and obligations on individuals.[8] The distinctiveness of the Treaty, as against other international Treaties to which the UK is party and which do not give rise to such rights, was much less apparent. Nevertheless, by passing the European Communities Act in 1972, (by a majority of eight votes on the Commons Second Reading), Parliament itself endorsed the incorporation of Community principles into domestic law. The terms of section 2(1) of the Act are worth replication,

'All such rights, powers, liabilities, obligations and restrictions from time to time created or arising by or under the Treaties, and all such remedies and procedures from time to time provided for by or under the Treaties as in accordance with the Treaties are without further enactment to be given legal effect or used in the United Kingdom shall be recognised and available in law, and be enforced, allowed and followed accordingly.'

On one view therefore, the operation of Community law in the UK involves no infringement of the principle of parliamentary supremacy at all. The status given to Community law is simply what Parliament has given it by statute. On the other hand, the traditional formulation of parliamentary sovereignty holds that Parliament cannot bind itself for the future. On that basis, it can be argued that Parliament remains entitled to pass a law inconsistent with the Community principles incorporated by the European Communities Act.

The traditional formulation is, however, difficult to reconcile with the jurisprudence of the ECJ. In *Costa v ENEL*[9] the ECJ asserted that transfer of the rights and obligations arising under the Treaty to the Community legal order by member states resulted in 'a permanent limitation of their sovereign rights, against which a subsequent national act incompatible with the concept of the Community cannot prevail'. Such considerations do, of course, raise highly charged political issues.

Assessing the supremacy of Community law: Three points seem particularly relevant in assessing the effect of the supremacy of Community law on the legislative process. First, there is the extent to which individually enforceable rights and obligations arise irrespective of domestic parliamentary involvement. Where this is the case, the domestic parliamentary process is sidelined (unless it can influence what comes forward from Europe in the first place). Second, there is the question of how British courts deal with situations that may require them to review Acts of Parliament that appear inconsistent with Community provisions. Such involvement goes beyond the traditional role of the courts which is one of interpretation and enforcement. The possibility of review by the courts inevitably raises implications for the processes by which law is made by Parliament. Third, it is necessary to consider to what extent the procedures for legislating on European issues, where Parliament does have an implementing role, depart from what would have been expected if the legislation had a domestic origin.

Regulations and directives: Reference has already been made to the individually enforceable nature of Treaty articles satisfying the ECJ's doctrine of direct effect.

The same doctrine applies to Community regulations. They can be parachuted into the domestic legal system without parliamentary involvement. On the other hand, implementation of directives does require the involvement of Parliament. The EC Treaty specifically provides that a directive 'shall be binding, as to the result to be achieved, upon each member state to which it is addressed, but shall leave to the national authorities the choice of form and methods'.[10] Directives are a very common European legislative tool and are particularly important for measures intended to harmonise the laws of member states.

The wording of the Treaty has not, however, prevented the development by the ECJ of a doctrine that directives are capable, at least in some instances, of conferring individually enforceable rights without further intervention by national authorities. Clearly, this doctrine is important in considering the extent to which Parliament can exercise oversight of practical implementation through its established domestic legislative processes. According to the criteria developed by the Court in a series of cases, if the obligations contained in a directive are sufficiently clear and exact to be capable of being applied directly by a national court, individually enforceable rights arise.[11] Such a directive can be relied upon by an individual against the member state to trump inconsistent national legislation provided the time limit for implementing the directive has expired. It should be noted though that application of the directly enforceable rights applies only to the individual against the state. The doctrine does not allow the state to argue that obligations are cast directly on individuals.

As a further step to ensure that member states do not benefit from failing to implement European legislation, the ECJ has gradually extended the definition of 'state'. So, for example, local authorities, health authorities and British Gas (when nationalised) have all been found by the ECJ to be emanations of the state.[12] As such, they are organisations against which individuals can invoke Community directives. This is true even though such bodies are in no way responsible for the failure of the national legislature (the narrow definition of 'state') to implement the directive pleaded against them. The consequence for the UK's legislative process is that Parliament's own input, through the 'choice of form and methods to secure implementation', is marginalised. Individuals may rely directly on the terms of directives against public bodies. The motivation to do that will arise if the terms of a directive are considered to be more favourable to an individual's case than the corresponding implementing national law. Avoiding such inconsistency ought to be an objective of the domestic legislative implementation process, if only to avoid the arbitrary distinction caused by the creation of legal rights which are exercisable against a public body but not against a private organisation.

Reviewing Acts of Parliament: The review of Acts of the British Parliament by the courts has perhaps attracted most attention politically and, undoubtedly, raises difficult constitutional questions. As with direct effect of Treaty articles, the doctrine of supremacy of Community law over the law of the member states has no basis in the founding Treaties. Rather, it has been developed by the ECJ as the basis on which the new legal order should operate. This new legal order is also the product of the Court's own decisions, beginning with *Van Gend en Loos* in which the Court found that member states had limited their own sovereign rights - an approach confirmed consistently since. According to the ECJ, the fact that a Community provision is considered to run counter to either fundamental rights as formulated by the constitution of a member state or the principles of a national constitutional structure does not affect the superior status of Community law.[13] So national courts must, according to the Court, give full effect to Community provisions, if necessary refusing by their own motion to apply any conflicting provision of national legislation, even if that has a specially elevated constitutional status in the member state.[14]

The position taken by the ECJ has the potential for wide-ranging consequences for the legislatures of all member states. It is, however, worth observing that the doctrine as enunciated by the Court does not actually require national courts to annul laws which conflict with Community provisions. Rather they should, according to the Court, suspend their operation where there are competing Community provisions that create individually enforceable rights. The Commission has argued that incompatibility of a subsequently enacted national law with Community provisions should result in the national law being treated as void. This argument has been rejected by the ECJ.[15] Its acceptance would, of course, have a far greater effect on national sovereignty than the doctrine of suspension of the operation of a national law in specific cases.

Ultimately, whatever the position taken by the institutions of the Community, acceptance of supremacy of Community law must depend on the acquiescence of the legal and constitutional guardians of each member state. When Parliament enacted the European Communities Act 1972, the decisions of the ECJ on the meaning of Community law were made authoritative in British courts.[16] The courts have accordingly been able to assert that the power to review Acts of Parliament rests on domestic authority rather than imposition from outside. There is little doubt from the domestic case law that the British judiciary takes this view. It is instructive to consider how conflicts have been approached in specific cases since the results undoubtedly have implications for the legislative process.

Extending supremacy; the *Factortame* case: *Factortame* is a leading case which has received a substantial political profile.[17] The case arose from the British government's desire to restrict the ability of fishing vessels controlled by foreign companies to access the British fish quota allocated under the Common Fisheries Policy. This was achieved by the Merchant Shipping Act 1988 (and associated regulations) which required 'genuine and substantial connection with the United Kingdom' before vessels could be registered for the UK quota.

Factortame, and other companies, were Spanish-controlled and could not fulfil the new requirements. They challenged the legislation as incompatible with the EC Treaty on grounds of discrimination by nationality and infringement of rights of companies to establishment in all member states. They sought an injunction restraining the government from imposing the new requirements while their contentions were being considered by the ECJ. The Court of Appeal ruled that it had no jurisdiction to grant interim relief disapplying an Act of Parliament. The House of Lords agreed. Lord Bridge noted that 'if the applicants [Factortame] fail to establish their case before the European Court, the effect of interim relief granted would be to have conferred in them rights directly contrary to Parliament's sovereign will'.[18]

The ECJ held that the offending provisions of the Merchant Shipping Act should be suspended pending a final determination of Factortame's claim. This ruling was accepted by the House of Lords and the injunction was granted. In doing so their Lordships were careful not to suggest that the result was an invasion of the sovereignty of Parliament. Others of a more political inclination took a quite different view.[19]

The case is of particular constitutional significance because it established the courts' ability to protect alleged rather than established rights under Community law and also their jurisdiction to grant interim relief by injunction against the Crown.

The case indicates the courts' increasingly explicit acknowledgement of the primacy of Community law. This acknowledgement was reinforced by the House of Lords' judgment in the *EOC* case.[20] Without referring the matter to the ECJ, the House accepted that the courts had jurisdiction to entertain an application for judicial review of provisions of the Employment Protection (Consolidation) Act 1978 governing part-time workers which the Equal Opportunities Commission considered to contravene Community provisions governing equalities.

Of course, none of these developments prevents Parliament from making laws. UK legislation that adversely affects only non-EU states or their citizens will not be challengeable on Community law grounds. Had the companies in Factortame been controlled by non-EU nationals the challenge would not have arisen. Nevertheless, much of the legislation produced by Parliament will have an impact on member states or their nationals in some form and as the European Union expands so the amount of legislation in this category will increase. Laws will simply need to be crafted to avoid incompatibility if the sort of difficulty which arose in Factortame is to be avoided. In one sense this does have the effect of limiting Parliament's freedom of action. It is, however, always open to Parliament to legislate so specifically and deliberately in conflict with Community provisions that the courts would feel bound to follow Parliament's will. The most obvious instance of that would be repeal of the European Communities Act 1972. Such action would, however, be essentially the result of political rather than legal or procedural developments dealt with in this article.

Implementing European initiatives: Finally, special mention should be made of the process applied when Parliament has a specific role to play in implementing European initiatives domestically. The principal instrument with which Parliament has such a role is the directive as national authorities are given the choice of form of methods to secure implementation. The European Communities Act 1972 provides for the implementation of Community obligations by means of Orders in Council or statutory instruments.[21] The Act makes clear that this method of implementation may be used even where enactment by primary legislation might otherwise be the procedural choice.

Plainly implementation by secondary legislation does not under existing parliamentary procedures enable the degree of scrutiny which can be applied through a parliamentary Bill. The use of secondary legislation no doubt reflects the practical reality of limited parliamentary time and the large number of Community instruments being generated. The EU Commission's Financial Services Action Plan, for example, has spawned over 40 directives aimed at securing a single market in those services.[22] In 2003 the Commons European Scrutiny Committee considered 1080 documents of which 26 were debated in standing committee and five on the floor of the House.[23] Directives may raise issues of general public importance which deserve scrutiny even if (as is the case under current procedures) the implementing statutory instrument cannot be amended. The changes to the weights and measures legislation which attracted considerable public attention as the result of the prosecution of shopkeepers for selling in imperial measures (the so-called 'metric martyrs' cases) were implemented by a statutory instrument that had been 21 minutes in standing committee.[24] Around half of that time had been taken by the minister's opening and closing remarks and backbench contributions accounted for about two minutes of the exchanges.[25]

The need to enhance the domestic scrutiny process for Community instruments is well recognised and has been acknowledged by the Foreign Secretary.[26] The European Union Committee of the House of Lords has considered the matter in detail.[27] Steps designed to improve the procedures by which domestic legislation implements directives and other Community instruments have already been taken and further action has been proposed. [28] Such action is certainly welcome as the possibility of over-implementation - 'gold plating' - is of continuing concern, not least in the financial services sector.[29] This concern is compounded by the effects on UK business of the failure by some member states properly to implement single market measures.[30] The recently established House of Lords Select Committee on the Merits of Statutory Instruments will look specifically at the appropriateness of the way EU legislation is implemented in specific cases.[31] The Commons Scrutiny Committee has also supported a government proposal for a Secondary Legislation Scrutiny Committee.[32] Such initiatives are clearly beneficial, particularly if the procedural arrangements encourage the submission of evidence by interested parties with a knowledge of the practical issues. The Commons Modernisation Committee is also considering how scrutiny of European issues might be enhanced and the creation of a committee which would cover all aspects of the EU's work. The government favours the creation of such a committee.[33]

Conclusion: Issues such as the way in which EU legislation is transposed into statutory instruments are important. Gold plating and the avoidance of over-enthusiastic enforcement by domestic agencies of laws that are enacted (which often seem to be behind complaints about European 'intrusion') are matters on which Parliament can have an important impact. Parliament needs, however, effectively to scrutinise proposals before they are adopted by the Community in legislative form. The extent to which the ECJ already regards Community legislation as conferring individual rights without further intervention by national Parliaments serves to emphasise the need for greater parliamentary involvement when policy is being developed. Failure to provide for it brings the danger that those who are affected by Community proposals will increasingly regard Parliament as 'outside the loop' and will therefore cease to regard it as relevant. Such marginalisation would plainly run wholly counter to the objective of enhancing democratic scrutiny.

Endnotes and references:

1   HC Deb 8/5/67, vol 746, col 108.
2   *Improving the Way the UK handles European Legislation:* Pilot Quality Assurance Study Synthesis Report, p2.
3   HC Deb, 22/7/04, vol 424, col 490W (explaining the basis for the figure in the report at reference 2 above).
4   Case 26/62, *NV Algemene Transport-en Expeditie Onderneming Van Gend en Loos v Nederlandse Administratie der Belastingen* [1963] ECR 1.
5   Article 25 (formerly Article 12).
6   The date specified in the Treaty of Accession.
7   Articles 39 and 43 (formerly 48 and 52), Articles 28-30 (formerly 20-36), Article 141 (formerly 119), Articles 81-82 (formerly 85-86).
8   For example *HC Deb*, 15 February 1972, vol 831, cols 270-272 (Second Reading of the European Communities Bill).
9   Case 6/64, *Costa (Flaminio) v ENEL* [1964] ECR 585.
10   Article 249 (formerly Article 189).
11   Case 41/74, *Van Duyn v Home Office* [1974] ECR 1337; Case 148/78, *Pubblico Ministero v Tullio Ratti* [1979] ECR 1629; Case 8/81, *Becker v Finanzamt Münster-Innenstadt* [1982] ECR 53.
12   Case 103/88, *Fratelli Costanzo SpA v Comune di Milano* [1989] ECR 1839, Case 152/84, *Marshall v Southampton and South West Hampshire Area Health Authority (Teaching)* [1986] ECR 723, Case C-188/89, *Foster and Others v British Gas* [1990] ECR I-3313. (British Gas was a nationalised industry when the cause of action arose.)
13   Case 11/70, *Internationale Handelsgesellschaft mbH v Einfuhr-und Vorratsstelle für Getreide und Futtermittel* [1970] ECR 1125.
14   Case 106/77, *Amministrazione delle Finanze dello Stato v Simmenthal SpA* [1978] ECR 629.
15   Cases C-10-22/97, *Ministero delle Finanze v IN.CO.GE '90 Srl* [1998] ECR I-6307.
16   European Communities Act 1972, s.2(4) and s.3.
17   *R v Secretary of State for Transport ex parte Factortame* [1990] 2 AC 85; (No 2) [1991] 1 AC 603.
18   *R v Secretary of State for Transport ex parte Factortame* [1989] AC 85, 143.
19   For example HC Deb, 20/6/90, vol 174, cols 923-4.
20   *R v Secretary of State for Employment, ex parte Equal Opportunities Commission and Another* [1994] 2 WLR 409.
21   Section 2(2) and section 2(4) of the Act. Schedule 2 to the Act lists certain matters such as increasing taxation which should be undertaken by primary legislation.

22   *Financial Services – Implementing the Framework for Financial Markets: Action Plan* (11/05/99) Com(1999)232.

23   European Scrutiny Committee (2003-04) *The Committee's Work in 2003* HC 42.

24   *Thoburn v Sunderland City Council and other cases* [2002] 3 WLR 247.

25   First Standing Committee on Statutory Instruments etc, 1/11/94.

26   HC Deb, 11/2/04, vol 417, col 1415.

27   House of Lords Select Committee on the European Union (2002-03) *Review of Scrutiny of European Legislation* HL15.

28   Transposition Guide: *How to Implement European Directives Effectively,* Cabinet Office (2003); Bellis R. *Implementation of EU Legislation: An Independent Study for the Foreign and Commonwealth Office,* Foreign and Commonwealth Office (2003).

29   See for example Association of Private Client Investment Managers and Stockbrokers *'The Gilded Cage' – Gold Plating EU Legislation into Law and Regulation* (May 2004).

30   House of Commons European Scrutiny Committee (2003-04) Thirtieth Report HC 42, para 10.

31   House of Lords Merits of Statutory Instruments Committee, *Special Report on the Committee's Methods of Working* (2003-04) HL 73, para 73-75.

32   House of Commons European Scrutiny Committee (2001-2) *European Scrutiny in the Commons,* HC 152, para 113. A subsequent letter from the Parliamentary Secretary Privy Council Office to the chairman of the Procedure Committee indicated a more cautious government approach to this proposal (House of Commons Procedure Committee (2003-03) Delegated Legislation: *Proposals for a Sifting Committee: the Government's Response to the Committee's First Report,* Annex A).

33   Select Committee on Modernisation of the House of Commons (2003-04) *Scrutiny of European Matters in the House of Commons: Government Memorandum from the Leader of the House of Commons* HC 508.

Paul Evans

Introduction: The European Convention on Human Rights (ECHR) was signed in 1950. In 1966 the right of individual petition to the Strasbourg Commission and Court of Human Rights was given to UK citizens by the then Labour Government. In 1998 another Labour Government introduced the Human Rights Act (HRA), which incorporated the Convention into UK law, and required the UK courts to interpret and give effect to the laws made by Parliament, so far as is possible, in a way which is compatible with the rights guaranteed in the Convention. Each of these developments has had a significant impact on the way that the Westminster Parliament makes law. This is particularly true of the last development, the incorporation of the ECHR into British law, which is recognised as creating a new constitutional relationship between the courts and Parliament. This chapter considers some implications for the legislative process of the major changes that have occurred in this area, looking particularly at the work of Parliament's Joint Committee on Human Rights (JCHR).

Although the Convention was not fully incorporated into UK law until 2000, it had bound the UK in international law since 1950, and there had been previous attempts to give Parliament a role in ensuring the compliance of domestic law with its provisions. In 1994 the House of Lords Liaison Committee had considered a proposal that the House should set up systems to check whether provisions in Bills complied with the European Convention on Human Rights and other human rights treaties, by extending the terms of reference of the (then) Delegated Powers Scrutiny Committee (DPSC), and to check secondary legislation for compliance, using either the Joint Committee on Statutory Instuments (JCSI) or the DPSC.[1] However, this proposal made no progress at the time.

From 1992 it was the declared intention of the Labour Party, if it was elected to government, to legislate for incorporation in domestic law of the rights guaranteed by the ECHR and this commitment was set out in its 1996 policy paper *Bringing Rights Home*.[2] However, there remained long-standing anxieties about the risks of handing powers to the courts to repudiate laws made by

Parliament. Following the 1997 general election, the White Paper of October 1997, *Rights Brought Home*, said,

'*Bringing Rights Home* suggested that 'Parliament itself should play a leading role in protecting the rights which are at the heart of a parliamentary democracy'. How this is achieved is a matter for Parliament to decide, but in the government's view the best course would be to establish a new Parliamentary Committee with functions relating to human rights ... The new Committee might conduct enquiries on a range of human rights issues relating to the Convention, and produce reports so as to assist the government and Parliament in deciding what action to take. It might also want to range more widely, and examine issues relating to the other international obligations of the United Kingdom such as proposals to accept new rights under other human rights treaties.'[3]

Proposals for a Joint Committee on Human Rights: The Human Rights Bill was introduced into the House of Lords in November 1997. On its Second Reading, the then Lord Chancellor (Lord Irvine) expressed his view that the Bill would,

'...deliver a modern reconciliation of the inevitable tension between the democratic right of the majority to exercise political power and the democratic need of individuals and minorities to have their human rights secured.'[4]

It was apparent that parliamentary mechanisms would have to be established in order to assess the provisions and implication of the Act on the legislative process. This was recognised by Lord Irvine who referred to the establishment of a specific committee,

'We have given very positive thought to the possibility of a parliamentary committee on human rights. This is not in the Bill itself because it would not require legislation to establish and because it would in any case be the responsibility of Parliament rather than the government. But we are attracted to the idea of a parliamentary committee on human rights, whether a separate committee of each House or a joint committee of both Houses. It would be a natural focus for the increased interest in human rights issues which Parliament will inevitably take when we have brought rights home.'[5]

During the Second Reading debate in the Commons, the Home Office Minister Mike O'Brien MP said,

'The government propose to strengthen Parliament's role by supporting the creation of a new parliamentary Committee on human rights ... If the House so decides, the Committee's function could be to scrutinise proposed legislation, to ensure that human rights are respected, to assess UK compliance with various human rights codes and to keep the Act - as it will eventually undoubtedly become - under constant review.'[6]

Margaret Beckett MP, then Leader of the House, confirmed to the Commons on 14 December 1998, after the Bill had received the Royal Assent, that a joint committee would be appointed. Subsequently, the Wakeham Commission on House of Lords Reform expressed the belief that after the implementation of the Human Rights Act it would be Parliament's duty to carry out proactive scrutiny of proposed primary and secondary legislation for human rights points and that the contribution of a specialist committee would be of 'crucial importance'.[7] The House of Lords agreed to the proposal in July 2000. After some delay in securing approval of the necessary motions in the Commons, the committee met for the first time on 31 January 2001.

The committee's remit as agreed by the two Houses was widely and permissively drawn - to consider and report on matters relating to human rights in the United Kingdom (but specifically excluding consideration of individual cases) - and it was also *required* to examine and report on remedial orders (a fast-track system for remedying incompatibilities in existing legislation identified by the courts).[8]

The Human Rights Act is carefully designed to protect parliamentary sovereignty, and to ensure that the courts cannot overturn laws made by the legislature. It does this in two ways. First, prospectively, section 19 of the Act requires a minister, when introducing a Bill into either House, to make a statement as to whether in his or her opinion the provisions of the Act are compatible with the Convention rights. In this way, Parliament should, to a great degree, be clear when passing a Bill that its intention is to legislate in a compatible manner (or occasionally, and with deliberation, in a manner which it is aware might be later found to be incompatible).

Second, and retrospectively, although the Act requires the courts to strive so far as possible to interpret the law in particular cases in a manner which is compatible with the Convention rights, where this proves impossible it does not allow the courts simply to repudiate the law. The law remains in force, but the court may make a 'declaration of incompatibility' (as the European Court of Human Rights had in the past been able to do). It is then up to the government to decide whether to introduce remedial legislation (using either the remedial order process or primary legislation). The JCHR is involved in advising Parliament on the operation of both prospective and retrospective provisions of the Act relating to and ensuring compliance.

Assessing government compliance: The examination of remedial orders is a duty placed upon the JCHR by the two Houses. In practice, this mechanism has been relatively little used: there have been only two such orders made. The examination of section 19 statements is not explicitly required of the Committee, but it agreed, early in its deliberations on how to interpret its wide-ranging remit, that it would give the first priority to examining Bills before the two Houses for compliance with the Convention rights. The dissolution of Parliament for the 2001 general election intervened before the Committee had really had a chance to get into its stride, but at the beginning of the 2001 Parliament, the new Committee reconfirmed the decision to give a high priority to this work.

The starting point for the scrutiny of the Joint Committee of Human Rights is the section 19 statement. The Committee looks at whether the minister's statement is well founded, and whether the Committee identifies any provisions in a Bill which, despite the opinion of the minister, it considers risks incompatibility. There are only three examples so far of section 19(1)(b) statements having been made by ministers, stating that a Bill is in their opinion likely to be incompatible with the Convention rights. The first was in relation to the Local Government Bill brought from the Lords in the 1999-2000 session after the Lords had removed the provision repealing 'section 28'. The second was on the Communications Bill in session 2002-03, partly in response to the JCHR's comments on the draft Bill that a blanket ban on broadcast political advertising might be found incompatible, but was nonetheless justifiable. The third was on the introduction of the Civil Partnerships Bill into the House of Commons in the 2003-04 session, after the Lords had amended it to extend its scope to certain family relationships.

The JCHR also decided to extend its scrutiny to Private Members' Bills, which do not require a section 19 statement, and to private Bills after a modified form of the section 19 procedure was applied to these through standing orders.[9]

Interference with Convention rights: The Committee will often agree with the minister that, although a provision interferes with a Convention right, the interference is justifiable, necessary and proportionate. Where it has doubts, the main grounds for a warning from the Committee could be:

- that a provision is self-evidently incompatible, and could not be given effect to in a compatible manner (clearly a very rare conclusion to reach);

- that a provision interferes with a Convention right, but the Committee doubts that the Government's claims of necessity and/or proportionality are well-founded;

- that a provision interferes with a Convention right, and the government has simply not presented evidence to support a claim of necessity;

- that a provision is not in itself incompatible, and may be justifiable in principle as a necessary interference with a Convention right, but that it is so wide in the discretion it allows that it could be used in an incompatible or disproportionate manner, and that safeguards against such use are insufficient (this is a very common ground for concern).

This list is not an exhaustive account of the sort of findings the Committee may make. But in general terms it adheres to the principle that its job is not to decide questions of compatibility but to warn the Houses that by making a certain law they risk being found to have legislated in a way that was incompatible with the Convention rights.

The remit of the Joint Committee on Human Rights: The Committee was set up as a response to the Human Rights Act, but the Act is nowhere mentioned in its terms of reference (except in relation to the definition of remedial orders). It has gradually developed a practice of giving more attention to issues connected with human rights instruments other than the ECHR, going beyond the strict testing of the section 19 statement. In this, it is following the jurisprudence of the European

Court of Human Rights, though it is not bound by it. Its remit makes no reference to scrutiny of legislation. However, by deciding to give priority to this work, the Committee has imposed on itself a role something akin to a 'scrutiny committee', rather like the Delegated Powers Committee of the Lords, the Joint Committee on Statutory Instruments or the European Scrutiny Committee of the House of Commons. It now has considerable experience of this kind of work, having at least glanced at every Bill introduced into either House in the three sessions since the general election. It has examined well over 300 Bills, and has drawn the special attention of each House to around 100 of these. Sometimes its reports have drawn to Parliament's attention relatively minor concerns about compliance; sometimes its concerns have gone to the heart of a Bill's purpose.

Examining Bills for compatibility: The Committee seeks to examine, with the assistance of its legal adviser, every government Bill at as early a stage as possible to determine whether significant questions of compatibility appear to be raised by any of its provisions. Where any such questions do appear to it to arise, a letter to the minister who made the section 19 statement is sent as soon as possible. The arguments underpinning such letters and the letters themselves are published as soon as practical in one of the Committee's regular progress reports. When the response from the minister is received, the Committee publishes its conclusions, sometimes accepting the arguments of the government, expressing itself persuaded by the evidence of necessity or the guarantees of proportionality, and sometimes concluding that it is unpersuaded. There may be further exchanges of correspondence as the Bill is making progress through the two Houses.

In the case of one draft Bill - the draft Gender Recognition Bill - the Committee was assigned as the principal pre-legislative scrutineer. In principle, the Committee seeks to treat the generality of draft Bills like the formal ones and examine them all in detail. The main difference in its practice in dealing with draft rather than formal Bills is that it feels no obligation to hear the government's case before reporting - relying on the fact that the government can respond when the Bill itself is introduced. The JCHR has an advantage over ad hoc joint committees considering draft Bills as it can reconsider the Bill as introduced in the light of its comments on the draft.

In the first session of the 2001 Parliament, the general practice of the Committee was to publish a stand-alone report on each Bill which raised substantive issues. From the 2002-03 session, it adopted the approach of making progress reports at the intermediate stages of its consideration, recognising the priority of getting comments before the Parliament and the wider public, but also bearing in mind the political pressure for a prompt response exerted by early publication of its concerns. It has continued to publish the occasional stand-alone report, often reflecting the human rights significance of a Bill (for example the Asylum and Immigration (Treatment of Claimants, Etc) Bill) or sometimes because it wishes to take a slightly more wide-ranging approach to a particular Bill (for example the Children Bill).

In her evidence to the Lords Constitution Committee's inquiry into the legislative process the chair of the JCHR, Jean Corston MP, expressed her belief that its work does affect the eventual outcome of the legislative process, both directly and indirectly. First, the growing awareness within government departments that each and every Bill will be examined by the Committee means that the human rights implications of proposed legislation are likely to be subject to specially anxious scrutiny by departmental lawyers and draftsmen and, where there are problems, it is more likely that they will be drawn to the attention of ministers before Bills are published. It is the *threat* of unavoidable, detailed and well-supported parliamentary scrutiny that is the key factor here in enhancing Parliament's influence on legislative outcomes.

Second, the Committee has had some, though not complete, success in persuading departments to give a fuller and more reasoned account of the Convention rights issues which they believe are engaged by particular provisions. The Committee argues that the Bill's explanatory notes should include the grounds for concluding that the provisions can be interpreted and given effect to in a compatible manner. In this, it is trying to engender a *culture of justification* within government, rather than allowing it to get away with a tradition of assertion. This culture of justification is enhanced and embedded by the way in which the Committee engages in continuing dialogue with departments through written (and occasionally oral) exchanges about provisions on which it has concerns, and through its post-legislative scrutiny of key provisions.

Third, by publishing its reports while Bills are making progress through the two Houses, there can be little argument that it has made a definite contribution to enhancing the quality of the debate that takes place on issues in proposed legislation relating to fundamental rights and freedoms. It is the quality and availability of independent, non-partisan evidence, information and advice to

Parliament (directed specifically to its needs) that enhances Parliament's capacity to influence the ultimate outcome of the legislative process. The effectiveness of the JCHR depends on the fact that its work is based on the legal and ethical foundation of the Convention, and to a lesser extent other human rights instruments. This provides a ready-made common ground for debate, and a framework for the rational resolution of differences.

Government responses: The Committee makes its warnings and it is then for each House to decide how to respond to them. It is in the fields of immigration, asylum and anti-terrorist legislation that the Committee has, perhaps inevitably, most often found itself in disagreement with the government's legislative proposals. If the government is obdurate, it is unlikely that the Bill will be substantially altered, though the government has often responded constructively to the Committee's comments. It altered, for example, some provisions of the Asylum and Immigration (Treatment of Claimants, Etc.) Bill, although the Committee was not entirely satisfied with the alternative. In contrast, it ignored the Committee's warnings about the effect of section 55 of the previous Immigration and Asylum Act (depriving asylum seekers who had not made a claim within 'reasonable time' of access to benefits) and a series of court decisions since the Act came into force have suggested that the Committee was probably correct in its assessment.

Post-legislative scrutiny: It is asserted that one shortcoming of the legislative processes of Parliament is its failure, institutionally, to consider the actual effects of the laws it makes. The JCHR does not have the resources to overcome this problem itself, although very often questions of compliance will only be tested in putting the law into practice. Its most sustained example of post-legislative scrutiny has been the Committee's work on Part 4 of the Anti-Terrorism, Crime and Security Act 2001 (which involved a derogation from the Convention rights with respect to the provisions for indefinite detention without trial of 'suspected international terrorists' who were not British citizens). The Committee reported on the annual renewal orders for this Part on each occasion on which they have been laid. Its 2004 report took into account the findings of the Newton Committee on the continuation of Part 4, and it followed this up with a further report on the Home Office review of counter-terrorism powers.[10]

The Committee's 2004 report on the meaning of 'public authority' under the Human Rights Act was perhaps an unprecedented example of Parliament taking on the courts over the interpretation of the intention of Parliament in making law.[11] This kind of sustained monitoring of what happens after legislation has been made is most unusual, and reflects the Committee's awareness of the anxiety within Parliament that the making of such a profound constitutional change as the Human Rights Act required a different level of monitoring of its impact.

Connecting with the public: The Committee's legislative scrutiny also helps to draw those outside Parliament into Parliament's law making process. Parliament on its own cannot protect people's human rights in the delivery of services, whether it concerns, for example, helping children in care, or providing humane treatment of the terminally ill. It can provide money, create and reorganise institutions and guide or direct them; but this only indirectly affects the experience of anyone who needs health care, or wants education, or wishes to be free from a fear of crime, or seeks better protection of whatever right they feel is threatened. A range of other bodies undertake work on these issues and because these bodies are concerned with different aspects of the protection of fundamental rights and freedoms, they increasingly recognise the role of the JCHR in getting these issues moved up the political agenda. Furthermore, they have increasingly seen providing evidence to it as a worthwhile exercise, which gives them a better chance to influence outcomes of the legislative process.

Conclusion: The Committee's effectiveness, like that of other committees, is often impeded by the pace at which legislation is taken through the Commons. The main problems lie in the shortness of the intervals between stages, and the very short times allowed for Report Stages, especially when substantial government amendments are introduced. Whether the Committee revisits a Bill at a later stage in the light of significant amendments is a decision coloured by both principle and happenstance. There usually needs to be some realistic chance of intervening at a stage before the Bill ceases to be amendable. It is this last condition which is often impossible to satisfy.

Three factors might be seen as providing lessons from the experience of the JCHR for Parliament's wider effectiveness in making the law. First is the grounding of its work in a clear set of agreed principles (however contested these may be in the wider political arena). Second is its ability to combine detailed technical scrutiny with a wider-ranging remit which enables it to consider the context in which the law is made, and the consequences which flow from making the law. Third is its ability to provide both Houses with well-informed and timely advice during the process of agreeing legislation.

Endnotes and references:

1   The proposal was based partly on Ryle M. 'Pre-legislative scrutiny: a prophylactic approach to protection of human rights (1994) *Public Law,* Sum 192-197, which itself owed something to Lord Lester of Herne Hill's maiden speech HL Deb 23/11/93, col 170.
2   The Labour Party *Bringing Rights Home* (1996).
3   Home Office *Rights Brought Home* (1997) Cm 3782.
4   HL Deb 3/11/97, vol 300 col 1234.
5   *ibid.*
6   HC Deb 16/2/98, vol 306 col 855.
7   *A House for the Future,* Royal Commission on Reform of the House of Lords (2000) chaired by Lord Wakeham, Cm 4534, para 5.32.
8   Made under section 10 and Schedule 2 of the Human Rights Act.
9   See S.O. 38(3) Commons and Lords and S.O. 169A(HC) and S.O. 98A(HL).
10 Joint Committee on Human Rights (2004) *Eighteenth Report - Review of Counter-terrorism Powers.* Privy Councillor Review Committee (2003-04) *Anti-terrorism, Crime and Security Act 2001 Review: Report,* HC 100 (the 'Newton Committee').
11 Joint Committee on Human Rights (2003-04) *The Meaning of Public Authority under the Human Rights Act,* HL 39 / HC 382.

11 | Regulation and the Legislative Process - Improving Scrutiny and Accountability

Neil Gerrard and Sam Hinton-Smith

Introduction: The rapid expansion in the number and powers of 'arms length' regulatory agencies in the past quarter century raises a number of major questions about the efficacy of mechanisms to scrutinise the actions of regulators, and to oversee the primary and secondary legislation which determines the extent and exercise of their powers. Given the crucial role that statutory regulators play in the success of the UK's economy in maintaining fair and competitive markets, and in protecting consumers, it is vital that proper mechanisms of parliamentary scrutiny are in place. Parliament must have sufficient authority to oversee effectively regulators' actions, and must also rigorously scrutinise legislation which establishes and extends the power of regulators.

The regulatory state: The number of regulatory bodies has mushroomed over the last 25 years. Governments of all political hues have sought to establish semi-independent executive agencies fulfilling various sectoral and departmental regulatory functions. The privatisation of utilities under the Conservative administrations of Margaret Thatcher and John Major was followed by the establishment of economic regulators overseeing the markets for telecommunications (1984), gas (1986), water (1989), electricity (1989/90) and railways (1993). This drive has continued since 1997, with the establishment of 'super regulators' such as the Financial Services Authority (FSA) and the Office of Communications (Ofcom). The present government has also sought to consolidate and enhance the power of existing bodies; for example, the Office of Fair Trading (OFT) was put on a statutory footing by the Competition Act 1998 and has been handed greater powers under the Enterprise Act 2002.

This process looks set to continue. The merger of the Inland Revenue and HM Customs and Excise, announced by the government in March 2004, will create another powerful super regulator, with significant powers of investigation and huge resources. Recent changes to company law audit requirements, introduced in the light of Enron and other corporate collapses, also herald significant expansion in the scope of regulatory law. Forthcoming corporate manslaughter legislation will mark a major step in the development of health and safety regulation.

The current debate over accountability and scrutiny: Current government priorities identify a strong regulatory framework as crucial to effective function of the economy and for the protection of consumers, employees and the environment. Major corporate scandals in the United States, such as Enron, WorldCom and Tyco, and in Continental Europe, such as Parmalat and Ahold, have provided the impetus for more robust regulatory structures across the globe. Britain has been no stranger to similar events; earlier corporate collapses such as BCCI, coupled with failures in corporate governance such as those at Equitable Life and Marconi, have highlighted the need for more rigorous systems in the UK. In particular, the move away from 'light touch' or self-regulation has accelerated since 1997.

The growth of regulators in the UK, and the consequent development of new centres of power outside Parliament, raises two major questions in relation to the role of Parliament. Firstly, is Parliament effectively fulfilling its role as a scrutineer of regulatory bodies? Secondly, are effective mechanisms in place to ensure that legislation, both primary and secondary, establishing and enhancing the powers of regulators, is being effectively scrutinised?

Regulator accountability - a democratic deficit? As the Hansard Society's Report, *Parliament at the Apex*, recognised, there is now a real concern that Parliament has failed to respond effectively to the growth of regulatory bodies and is failing to ensure that they are properly accountable to parliamentarians.[1] Peter Riddell argued in his book *Parliament Under Blair*,

'Parliament has failed to cope with the growth of alternative centres of power. The formation of Next Steps executive agencies, the creation of regulators for the privatised utilities ... all have far reaching implications for accountability. The official line that these bodies are still accountable, via ministers, to Parliament is an unconvincing and inadequate description of the real position.'[2]

Increasingly, other sectors such as the media, consumer groups and regulated businesses are regarded as more effective scrutinisers. Sir Ian Byatt, former

Director of Ofwat, has pointed to the role of the media and pressure groups, saying, 'increasingly it is these who are leading the process of scrutiny and challenging the accountability of government'.[3] Moreover, many regulators' primary concern is the threat of legal challenges from the regulated community which might overturn their decisions, rather than democratic scrutiny.

The House of Lords Constitution Committee, chaired by Lord Norton of Louth, recently published the findings of its inquiry into the accountability of regulators.[4] The Committee made a number of welcome recommendations, including the establishment of a joint parliamentary committee to scrutinise regulatory bodies, and greater parliamentary scrutiny of the regulators' annual reports and published Regulatory Impact Assessments (RIAs). It also made a number of key recommendations to improve the drafting of regulatory legislation. Firstly, it suggested that regulatory legislation should be drafted in close consultation with regulators to achieve clearly defined objectives. It also recommended that the proposed parliamentary committee on regulation should be consulted over any proposal to confer statutory powers on a new regulator, or to add to those of an existing regulator.

The government has gone some way towards recognising the current problems identified by Lord Norton and his Committee. In response to the report, the government has acknowledged the need for a higher level of parliamentary scrutiny over regulatory bodies, and intends to encourage regulatory authorities to take steps to ensure higher levels of scrutiny. It also plans to increase regulatory transparency and further the principles of good regulation and effective accountability by encouraging regulators to make documents such as RIAs, plans and other such relevant materials publicly available. In addition, it has promised to work with sectoral regulators to encourage them to follow its Code of Practice when undertaking consultation exercises. However, the government has rejected some of the proposed methods of increasing scrutiny advocated by the Lords committee. Most notably, it will not grant the National Audit Office oversight over the finances of some regulatory bodies, such as the Financial Services Authority, and it has rejected calls to revise the current audit and appeals process. Finally, the government has declined to press for the creation of a parliamentary committee to scrutinise the regulatory bodies, though this in theory remains a matter for the Houses of Parliament.

In short, the Lords inquiry has found there is a shortfall in the democratic accountability of UK regulators. The deficiency also extends to legislative scrutiny affecting the regulatory sector.

The legislative process and the regulators: The recent expansion of the state's regulatory functions raises a further issue which is inextricably linked with the Hansard Society's *Issues in Law Making* series - how legislation which establishes and enhances the powers or regulators is scrutinised. Given the extensive powers that regulators wield - including quasi-criminal powers of investigation and enforcement - it is crucial that Parliament properly scrutinises both primary and secondary legislation relating to UK regulators.

A raft of legislation establishing or enhancing the powers of various regulatory bodies has been passed since 1997. For example, the powers of the Office of Fair Trading (OFT) have been enhanced by the Competition Act 1998 and the Enterprise Act 2002. As well as introducing severe criminal penalties for those found guilty of breaching it, the Enterprise Act gave the OFT extensive powers to enter premises with a warrant, to take possession of relevant documents, to require answers to questions and to conduct covert surveillance. As noted above, the UK's first super regulator, the Financial Services Authority, was established under the Financial Services and Markets Act 2000. The Act created a financial regulator with substantial powers of search and seizure. More recently, the Office of Communications (Ofcom) was set up under the Communications Act 2002. Looking ahead, it is likely that primary legislation will be introduced in the near future enshrining the powers of the new combined revenue raising authority, following the merger between the Inland Revenue and HM Customs and Excise. It is essential that the legislation establishing such an important body is properly scrutinised and that its structure and powers are sound and robust.

The advent of pre-legislative scrutiny: There have been several welcome developments in this area, such as the use of pre-legislative scrutiny on major pieces of regulatory legislation. Before the Financial Services and Markets Bill was considered by Parliament, a draft Bill was published by the Treasury. The financial services industry, the public and three parliamentary committees[5] were given the opportunity to comment on the draft legislation before it was put before Parliament. The Financial Services and Markets Bill was the first Bill to be considered in draft by a Joint Committee of both Houses of Parliament. Indeed, there were many distinctive features of the Bill's passage. The Bill was firstly examined by the House of Commons Treasury Select Committee, before its examination by the Joint Committee of both Houses. It was the first significant piece of legislation which needed to be certified by ministers as compatible with the European Convention on Human Rights. Additionally, it was the first public Bill to be subject to the carry-over procedure, allowing its passage to span two parliamentary sessions.[6]

The work of a joint committee of the Commons and the Lords, established specifically to scrutinise the draft legislation, was especially significant, holding seven oral evidence sessions and examining some 60 written submissions. Moreover, in being given a specific remit that included scrutinising the proposed arrangements for the accountability of the FSA, the joint committee was also able to examine options for the ongoing parliamentary scrutiny of the FSA. This procedure allowed concerns and practical issues to be raised and incorporated into the process.

A joint committee of both Houses was also establish to undertake pre-legislative scrutiny of the Communications Bill. Once again, the process featured an important innovation in the form of a Hansard Society-moderated online consultation between interested parties and the public and the parliamentary committee that was scrutinising the Bill. It was the first online consultation to consider a specific piece of legislation in draft form and its success can be seen by the fact that two of the committee's key policy recommendations came directly from suggestions made on the forum.

In addition, regulators wield significant powers under delegated legislation. As Alex Brazier demonstates in the chapter on delegated legislation, there is a major shortfall in Parliament's scrutiny of statutory instruments. This is of particular concern in the case of regulators, because of the major powers they have under delegated legislation. For example, the Financial Services and Markets Act contained considerable powers for the provision of secondary legislation, to allow for flexibility and to ensure that the law did not become outdated. The House of Lords Delegated Powers and Legislation Committee expressed concern over the extensive statutory powers, totalling more than 80, given to the FSA to initiate secondary legislation. The committee recommended the formation of a parliamentary committee to review the FSA's annual report and to take regular evidence from a wide range of interests including consumers and practitioners.

A greater role for departmental select committees in the scrutiny of legislation - one of the Hansard Society's key recommendations in relation to improving the scrutiny functions of standing committees - would ensure better scrutiny of major legislation which establishes new regulatory bodies. Such an enhanced role for select committees would also ensure greater scrutiny of efforts to grant more powers to existing regulators. Moreover, this would enable those select committee members responsible for holding specific regulators to account for the exercise of their executive functions to have a major influence on any legislation amending or enhancing these powers. The scrutiny of executive functions and of proposed changes to legislation should go hand in hand.

Conclusion: Mechanisms to scrutinise both the passage of regulatory legislation and the executive actions of regulators are frequently inadequate. Conventional means of legislative scrutiny are insufficient given the impact of legislation which establishes arms length regulators with wide-ranging powers. At the same time, mechanisms to hold regulators to account are unsystematic and haphazard and do not always best reflect or respond to the interests of consumers, businesses, and voters. As demonstrated elsewhere in this publication, Parliament frequently lacks the necessary means and authority to act as an effective scrutiniser.

However, a number of recent developments suggest that parliamentary scrutiny in this area is improving. The introduction of pre-legislative scrutiny, as used in the consideration of the Financial Services and Markets Bill, has given Parliament a greater opportunity to oversee the passage of legislation which grants regulators wide-ranging powers. Moreover, it has presented an opportunity for other interested parties outside Parliament to bring greater influence over the legislative process; for example, consumers, · academics, campaigning organisations, regulated businesses and their professional advisers, including the legal profession.

Additional developments in this area, such as the introduction of formal means to conduct post-legislative scrutiny, would further enhance Parliament's ability to oversee regulatory legislation. A specific role for departmental select committees to undertake post-legislative reviews would allow committee members to use their experience and expert knowledge to consider in depth the implementation of legislation. In addition, we should look to emulate global best practice, such as the use of parliamentary select committees to vet senior regulatory appointments and consider secondary legislation in detail. Such reforms would not only facilitate effective parliamentary oversight of regulators' actions; they would also ensure that regulatory bodies have sufficient powers and resources to fulfil their required role. The imperative to provide regulators with powers that are both effective and proportionate has never been greater.

Endnotes and references:

1   Brazier A. *Parliament at the Apex, Parliamentary Scrutiny and Regulatory Bodies,* Hansard Society (2003).

2   Riddell P. *Parliament under Blair* London (2003).

3   Evidence to Hansard Society Committee on Parliamentary Scrutiny, *The Challenge for Parliament: Making Government Accountable* (2001) chaired by Lord Newton of Braintree, Hansard Society.

4   House of Lords Committee on the Constitution, *The Regulatory State: Ensuring its Accountability* (2003-04) HL68-I.

5   The three committees were a Joint Committee of the Commons and the Lords that was established to examine the proposed legislation, the Treasury Select Committee and the House of Lords Delegated Powers and Deregulation Committee.

6   Smith-Hughes A. *Parliament, The City and Financial Regulation: a review of the passage of the Financial Services and Markets Act 2000* Hansard Society (2000).

12 | Law in Practice

Vanessa Knapp

Introduction: The law affects each of us every day in almost everything we do. It sets out our rights and responsibilities as spouse, parent, child, employee or employer, and the consequences of speeding, stealing or physical violence; it regulates what happens when we buy food, a television set or house and what happens to our property when we die; and it provides ways of resolving disputes. 'Ignorance of the law is no excuse', but in practice it is impossible to know and understand all the laws which may affect us. So individuals and organisations with plans or problems need specialists, solicitors and barristers, to explain the applicable laws and their impact. Often this is difficult for lawyers to do, because of uncertainty or complexity in the relevant Act of Parliament or statutory instrument. Such difficulties are not inevitable, however, and this chapter examines some of the ways in which legislation could be improved.

Given the importance of law in our daily lives and the significant ways in which it affects us, we need to have 'good laws'. But what does this mean in practice? Three important components are that laws should be: clear, readily accessible and up-to-date.

Clear law: Legislative clarity involves two things: being clear about what the law is intended to achieve (its aims) and expressing those aims in plain English. Being clear about the policy can be difficult in practice. Many laws seek to balance competing interests, for example, the differing interests of an employer and an employee. Whilst it may be easy to set out a basic principle, it is harder to foresee all the circumstances in which that principle may be applied and decide whether it will work appropriately. Increasingly, when determining policy, the government considers whether the benefits will outweigh the potential costs on those who have to comply. This is particularly important in the commercial world where English law 'competes' with the laws of other countries to make this an attractive place to do business.

Writing laws as clearly and as simply as possible would help users. The style of drafting laws has changed over the years, but also differs from one piece of legislation to another. Often, clarity is not helped by the fact that a new law is amending an existing one, which may be quite old and use expressions which are no longer common. However the change has to fit with the existing law and the way it is drafted. Usually there will not be enough time available to redraft the whole Act. Changing the existing wording, which the courts may have considered and given a particular meaning to, may also raise doubts about whether the new wording has the same meaning as the old wording or is intended to indicate a change in the law.

The Tax Law Re-write Project is a good example of an initiative to deal with such problems. The project was established following an Inland Revenue report to Parliament in 1995 on simplifying the UK tax system. The overall aim is to re-write the UK direct tax primary legislation to make it clearer and easier to use, without changing the law. So far, two Acts have been re-written and PAYE regulations have been made. The project has a steering committee and consultative committee as well as a project team. The project publishes an annual plan which reviews its progress and sets out its plans for the next year. The project publishes draft clauses for consultation and carries out structured consultation on particular topics with specialist groups.[1]

Another problem arises when EU directives are implemented into English law. (The chapter by Paul Double, *The Impact of European Community Law on the British Legislative Process*, looks at the impact of Europe on British legislation.) The words and concepts used in directives often do not equate to those that English law recognises. This poses a challenge; how to 'translate' the directive into English law without inadvertently imposing more onerous requirements. Robin Bellis has suggested various ways in which this challenge could be met in an independent report commissioned by the Secretary of State for Foreign and Commonwealth Affairs.[2]

Readily accessible: It should be easy for users to find the law that affects them in a particular area. However, in practice this is often very difficult. The relevant provisions may be set out in Acts of Parliament, statutory instruments and codes or guidance. For any one area there may well be more than one Act, many statutory instruments, several codes (which may be updated regularly) and extensive guidance. The internet could help make this material more accessible by hyperlinking related pieces of information together, such as an Act of Parliament to all the statutory instruments made under it.

It is vital that Acts and statutory instruments are publicly available when, or before, they come into force (some statutory instruments have not been available until a later date). Ideally, however, both Act and regulations should be available before then, to allow advisers time to read and consider them, and to advise those who are planning to do something which will be affected by the change. Changes in law sometimes mean that individuals or businesses will need to make changes to the systems they have in place. For example, an employer may need to change their safety procedures to meet a new requirement. This may take time and it is helpful to have a delay between the law being enacted and coming into force. A good example of an initiative which helps business is the Department of Trade and Industry's commitment to introduce employee regulations on just two dates in each year.

Up-to-date: 'Good law' also reflects the current needs of society. This means that the law must be kept under review to see if there are provisions which have become obsolete and to see if there are developments which need to be taken into account. The following two examples may help to illustrate this.

When the law relating to holding meetings of shareholders was originally written it was usual for all shareholders to meet in one location. If they were not able to attend the meeting in person, they could appoint someone else to attend in their place by posting a form to the company. Today, when large companies have shareholders all around the world it is unlikely that they will all want to assemble in one location, and the company may be happy to have a meeting in places outside the UK at the same time as the meeting takes place in the UK, using satellite technology. Shareholders also expect to be able to appoint someone else to attend the meeting using fax, email or some other form of electronic communication. The Companies Act has been amended to deal with the latter point, whilst the recent Company Law Review considered in detail how the law of meetings should be brought up-to-date.

A second instance of the law not keeping up-to-date with changes in society concerns unmarried couples. According to the Office of National Statistics, in 2001-02 a quarter of unmarried men and women in Britain lived together and, extrapolating from their figures, 24 per cent of babies were born out of wedlock. Of these births, the vast majority are registered by both parents who live at the same address. Many such couples wrongly assume that they have similar legal rights to those who are married but in fact the law treats them differently. The Law Society, as part of the law reform work it undertakes, has urged the government to change the law so that all couples (whether of the same or opposite sex), living together for a substantial period or who have had a child together are not disadvantaged as a result of their cohabitation.[3]

So far, this chapter has looked at the main elements of 'good law'. The rest of this chapter considers various approaches which could help to ensure that new laws are 'good laws'.

Wide consultation: The first thing to do is to identify whether a new law is needed and, if so, why and what it should achieve. Lawyers can be very helpful in this process. From their experience of advising clients they have first hand experience of the areas which regularly cause problems and the reasons why, and also areas where problems arise but where the law does not provide a helpful solution – for example when an unmarried couple separates. As, over time, they advise clients with differing views and interests, for example both landlords and tenants, they can contribute a balanced perspective. The Law Commission also has an excellent reputation for reviewing the law and recommending reform.

The Company Law Review: The Company Law Review, which was launched in March 1998 and produced its final report in June 2001, is an excellent example of a process which worked well. It reviewed the existing law, identifying the problems companies faced both from the existing law and in areas where there was no law, and made proposals both on policy matters and more detailed points. The purpose of the review was to create a framework which promoted the competitiveness of British companies, struck a proper balance between the interests of those concerned with companies, and promoted consistency, predictability and transparency in the law. There were also clear guiding principles for the review, including that company law should be primarily enabling.

One of the principal reasons for the Review's success was its working methods. Working groups were established to review all the major areas. These comprised a wide range of interested parties, from representatives of companies, employees and shareholders to accountants, lawyers and other advisers, who brought expertise and access to other organisations and networks with a keen interest in the matters being reviewed. Group discussions helped to identify problems and possible solutions. The major issues were analysed and proposed solutions were put forward in a series of consultation papers which gave the public sufficient time to consider them and to express their views. In some cases particular areas were considered again in later consultations in the light of responses. The review's final report set out its main recommendations and included some illustrative draft clauses. One of the benefits of this approach was that almost all of the proposals were supported by a substantial majority of respondents. The involvement of such a wide group of people should also mean that the government will continue to receive informed and constructive comments when it publishes the proposed new Companies Bill.

Allow sufficient time: Allowing sufficient time is a crucial part of the process needed to create 'good laws'. As the Company Law Review shows, reviewing a large area of law and making proposals which will stand the test of time can be a lengthy process. It is also important to ensure that there is enough time at each stage. For example, much of the benefit of a good review process will be lost unless sufficient time is also allowed to consult on draft legislation, including any statutory instruments to be laid. The draft regulations relating to community interest companies were published by the Department of Trade and Industry while the Companies (Audit, Investigations and Community Enterprise) Bill was still being considered which helped inform debate on the relevant provisions in the Bill.

Lawyers can be particularly useful in commenting on both early proposals and the wording of draft legislation, especially in technical areas. Through its specialist committees, this has been an important aspect of the work of the Law Society for many years, one example being the recommendations on unmarried couples mentioned earlier. Practitioners have a good understanding of the existing law and can help to identify proposed wording which will not work (either at all or as intended) or which will create uncertainty (for example because it changes wording that the courts have interpreted in a particular way). They may also be able to suggest areas which have not been covered but need to be, or areas where change is needed or which will be difficult to implement in practice.

Parliamentary time: Time pressures are felt particularly keenly in Parliament. As the amount and complexity of legislation increases, there is often insufficient time to consider the wording in great detail. If Parliament is trying to settle both policy and wording at the same time this can lead to unsatisfactory results. Part IV of the Companies Act 1989 on registration of company charges, for example, was inserted during the Act's passage through Parliament but has never been implemented because it became apparent that it would be unworkable in practice. The area is now being reconsidered. It can also be difficult to find parliamentary time to amend existing legislation, even if it is agreed that the amendments are needed and the wording is uncontroversial. For example, the Public Offers of Securities Regulations 1995 contained errors not corrected until 1999.

These problems have led to consideration of whether parliamentary time can be used more efficiently and whether the use of different types of legislation can contribute to this process. In some areas, a prior review of the existing law and consultation on the proposed policy and draft clauses can do a great deal to reduce the amount of parliamentary time needed to consider a provision, whilst also providing reassurance that the proposals have been carefully considered.

Secondary legislation: The form of legislation chosen can also help achieve more effective use of parliamentary time and offer a better chance of being able to amend the law when this is needed. Generally, it is easier to amend statutory instruments than Acts of Parliament and they are often an appropriate form of legislation for more technical areas which may need to be changed quite frequently. As explained above, wherever possible the statutory instrument dealing with a particular topic should be available at the same time as the provision in the draft primary legislation which gives the power for that area to be dealt with by secondary legislation. This should help to ensure that the power in the primary legislation is sufficiently broad, and also that any necessary safeguards or conditions for its use are imposed. However, there are drawbacks to the use of secondary legislation. For example, unlike primary legislation, secondary legislation cannot generally be amended during debate and must be passed as it stands or completely rejected. Further, a statute supplemented by a long series of amending regulations can be very difficult to understand.

Soft law: In some cases, it may be better not to legislate, but to deal with a topic by allowing another body to make rules or adopt a code. One of the advantages of this non-legislative, or 'soft law', approach, apart from avoiding the need for precious parliamentary time, is that it offers flexibility and can take a variety of forms. For instance, a group may be created which has specialist knowledge of the areas to be dealt with and can keep the rules or code up-to-date. In the company law field, for example, the Financial Reporting Council has published the Combined

Code on Corporate Governance. Although not directly binding on UK companies, companies whose shares are listed must either comply with the Code or explain why they have not done so. It is generally thought that this 'comply or explain' approach to corporate governance has been very successful in raising standards.

Soft law can therefore play an important role, but it too has its drawbacks. Amongst them are that its status may be unclear and it may be hard to access, whether on the internet or on paper. Furthermore, over the years, the body of soft law in an area may be considerable and, unless regularly pruned, may become unmanageable.

Where rules or a code are appropriate, proper consultation beforehand and ready accessibility are just as important as for legislation. There was wide consultation of interested parties and a healthy debate before the Financial Reporting Council adopted the Combined Code. As corporate governance is an area where expectations have been changing fairly quickly, it has been helpful to have a process which allows the Code to keep up with the expectations of companies, investors and other interested groups.

Regular updating: Keeping the law up-to-date is another important aspect of making 'good law'. Following the Company Law Review, the Department of Trade and Industry is proposing a new approach to restating and reforming company law. It is suggesting a special form of secondary legislation to increase the flexibility and accessibility of company law in future. This will allow it to amend and reform the law more easily as and when it becomes necessary or desirable (for example to take into account developments in European law) and to restate the existing law in order to simplify and clarify it, but without changing its effect. In view of the wide powers proposed, the procedure would include consultation with interested parties and representative organisations; an explanatory document to accompany the draft legislation which would set out the purpose, intended benefits and the results of the consultation process; a 60 day period for parliamentary scrutiny, and a requirement for both Houses of Parliament to debate and approve the final draft order. Minor, technical, routine or regular changes to the law could still be dealt with using existing powers.

Conclusion: Too much legislation is still difficult to follow, hard to find, and frustrating to apply, even for lawyers. Legislation does not need to present such problems, which result in much wasted time and money and possibly protracted uncertainty for lawyers and clients alike. Significant progress towards 'good law' has already been made through, for example, increased use of draft Bills. More could be done through structural changes such as improving the consultative processes, pre-legislative and parliamentary scrutiny and by paying more attention to formal aspects such as drafting and design techniques, and to the best ways of making legislation available to the user. The goal is legislation which is clear, kept up-to-date, works well in practice and is as user-friendly and accessible as possible. We each have a keen interest in making sure that the laws which govern us achieve these aims.

Endnotes and references:

1   More information on the project is available at www.inlandrevenue.gov.uk/rewrite.
2   Available at www.fco.gov.uk/Files/kfile/EUBellis.pdf.
3   The Law Society's Better Law Making Programme aims to encourage government and political parties to build on reforms already instituted and continue improving the law making process. During the Programme the Law Society has welcomed the opportunity to work closely with the Hansard Society.

13 | Parliament, Government and the Politics of Legislative Reform

Declan McHugh

Introduction: Parliament performs two important, but potentially contradictory, roles. One is to sustain the executive by giving assent to its legislative programme, the other is to scrutinise the executive and hold it to account between general elections.[1] The focus of this chapter is on recent reforms to the former function: the legislative process. But in looking at legislative reform in the context of parliamentary modernisation, it is necessary to consider the second of Parliament's central roles: scrutiny of the executive. This is because it is government that proposes most of the legislation, which Parliament subsequently carries, amends or opposes. In practice Parliament's role in the law making process is limited to examining and improving government proposals. In so doing, as Koen Muylle notes, Parliament 'controls an act of the executive'.[2] Consequently, when identifying Parliament's functions, law making cannot be divorced from parliamentary control because, as Pierre Avril observes, scrutinising legislation is a way for Parliament to control the government.[3]

There is, then, a crucial political dimension to the operation of the legislative process. In the British political system, the executive both comes from, and requires the support of, a majority in Parliament. In normal circumstances a government with a workable majority in the House of Commons can rely upon its backbenchers to support the Bills it brings to Parliament and to reject amendments to those Bills suggested by opposition parties that the executive is unwilling to accept. In practice British governments have appeared generally unwilling to accede to opposition amendments for reasons other than a strict evaluation of the quality or value of the amendments. According to Muylle, that 'unwillingness can be explained by a certain pedantry, but it can also be due to the need to have a Bill adopted by a certain date, especially in bicameral systems, where adopting amendments in the second chamber usually means that it will be sent back to the first chamber or to a [committee], causing delay in its adoption. Attempts to improve the effectiveness of parliamentary legislative procedures are thus often discarded because of political imperatives.'[4]

Labour's commitment to reform: Yet, the Labour Government elected in 1997 appeared unequivocal about its determination to make Parliament 'a more effective and efficient legislature', as part of its broader agenda of 'national renewal', outlined in the party's election manifesto. It promised to transform Britain into 'a country with drive, purpose and energy' declaring that, 'In each area of policy a new and distinctive approach has been mapped out, one that differs from the old left and the Conservative right. This is why new Labour is new. New Labour is a party of ideas and ideals but not of outdated ideology. What counts is what works. The objectives are radical. The means will be modern.'[5]

The Westminster Parliament was thus braced for the impact of Labour's future wave. In 1996, Ann Taylor MP, Shadow Leader of the House of Commons, had foreshadowed the party's plans for institutional renewal in a speech to Charter 88, fashionably entitled, 'New Politics, New Parliament'. Significantly, her vision of parliamentary reform was not concerned with domestic issues such as sitting hours and office accommodation but focussed on the more fundamental challenge to 're-establish the proper balance between Parliament and the executive'.[6] Her speech delighted an audience that believed fundamental parliamentary reform was long overdue and echoed sentiments expressed by Richard Crossman, as Labour Leader of the House, three decades earlier. On that occasion, in a Commons debate on his proposals to set up select committees, Crossman had drawn a distinction between 'modernisation', which he equated with 'housekeeping' matters such as measures to equip Parliament with more effective voting systems or better loudspeakers, and 'reform', which he associated with changes to the core functions of Parliament in order to shift the balance of power from the executive towards the legislature: the efficiency of the legislative process; the time allotted for debate; and the opportunity for scrutiny of the executive. He argued that reform was of far greater importance than modernisation, though he sought to address both.[7]

The establishment of the Modernisation Committee: Taylor's speech to Charter 88 suggested that what she sought was consistent with Crossman's earlier approach. Substance, not style, would characterise Labour's modernisation programme with the party focussing on improving Parliament's capacity to produce better legislation by enabling MPs to hold the executive more effectively to account. 'Those tasks will be Labour's true project for Parliament and, awkward though it may appear to a few on our side, a more accountable government is a better government and ultimately a more re-electable government.'[8] As the writers of *Yes, Minister* might have put it, such a clear commitment to strengthen Parliament was 'courageous'. Governments do not generally choose to make life harder for themselves.

Labour's election manifesto nonetheless reaffirmed the party's conviction that the House of Commons was in need of strengthening through a process of modernisation and promised to establish a designated select committee for the purpose. Following the party's landslide election victory, a Select Committee on the Modernisation of the House of Commons was duly established and the scene was set for 'New' Labour to create a 'New' Parliament. However, opponents of the government were soon concerned that the modernisation programme could yet be deflected off course or even directed to opposite ends. Somewhat controversially, the chair of the new Modernisation Committee was to be the Leader of the Commons. This was an unusual step in that select committees of the House are not generally chaired by members of the executive and the move was consequently greeted by reformers with a degree of scepticism. The House nevertheless unanimously supported the creation of the Modernisation Committee, although several Conservative and Liberal members voiced their fears that the government would be more concerned to use its enormous majority to smooth the passage of its extensive legislative programme.

Having the Leader of the Commons as chair of the Modernisation Committee was seen as a double-edged sword.[9] On the one hand, she could act as an enabling force – a powerful figurehead inside the Cabinet arguing the case for reform, making it much more likely that the committee's proposals would be accepted and implemented. On the other, the close involvement of a member of the executive, ultimately more concerned to guard the government than to strengthen Parliament, could see the Modernisation Committee diverted off an agenda of increasing accountability towards one concerned with improving parliamentary efficiency.

It was because opposition parties were keenly aware of the 'political imperatives' that they viewed Labour's modernisation agenda with some unease. Their discomfort was made all the more acute by the size of the government's majority in the Commons: 179 – the largest since 1935. The sense of powerlessness that this instilled in opposition MPs was memorably captured in the remark of one Conservative Member, who compared the sight of the 418 Labour MPs assembled on the green benches to 'that scene from Zulu'.[10] Moreover, opposition MPs were conscious that Labour would be anxious to implement its manifesto without obstruction. As Ann Taylor told the House, 'the legislative programme of a new government who have been out of office for 18 years is particularly heavy in the first year'.[11] In such circumstances, Conservatives and Liberal Democrats feared, the government would become increasingly 'executive-minded'.[12]

Initial proposals for change: However, fears that the government's commitment to strengthen Parliament would give way to more narrow self-interest were partly assuaged by the publication, in July 1997, of the first Modernisation Committee report on the legislative process. Significantly, the report had been produced in very quick time – just a few months after Labour's election victory – suggesting that the Leader of the House, and the committee that she chaired, meant business. The main themes of that report included proposals to introduce programme motions for the timetabling of Bills; pre-legislative scrutiny and draft Bills; flexible scrutiny of Bills; more explanatory notes on Bills; and the carry-over of public Bills into the following session.[13] The committee decided not to take oral evidence during the course of its inquiry but to rely instead on evidence from existing reports and written submissions. This approach led some MPs to criticise the report for lack of novel radicalism. However many interested observers thought the report contained a number of sensible recommendations that, if properly implemented, could improve the legislative process.[14] The ingredients looked right, but as the example of programming of legislation soon served to illustrate, not enough attention had been paid to the blending.

As Alex Brazier has described elsewhere in this book, programming was intended as a means to introduce a more rational approach to the legislative timetable, allow more effective and consistent scrutiny of proposed legislation, and to give the opposition a fairer opportunity to debate and vote on the parts of a Bill they wished to address. All the while it was recognised that the government had a proper right and expectation to get its legislation passed in reasonable time. The idea of programming was not a new idea. It had been advocated by reformers for several years - notably in *Making the Law* - as a mechanism that could enable legislation to pass through Parliament without resort to the 'guillotine' and in a more transparent fashion than the opaque timetabling procedure known as the 'usual channels'.[15] However, despite being introduced with unanimous support, growing discontent and divisions between the parties about the way programming was being used in practice undermined that initial mood of consensus. The Conservatives soon argued that the government was using programme motions in a way that made it 'easier...to get its legislative programme through the House, and, in so doing lessen, rather than encourage proper and adequate scrutiny'.[16] Interestingly this was not a simple government-opposition spat; senior Labour backbenchers also criticised the use of programming, typified by Gwyneth Dunwoody MP bluntly telling the House that 'those who talk about timetabling Bills do Back Benchers, irrespective of their party and certainly of the rubbish that goes on, a great disservice'.[17]

Changes without coherence: The effective failure of programming to work out as originally intended provides an instructive insight into the basic failings that weakened the impact of Labour's strategy to modernise Parliament. The fundamental problem was that, once in office, the Labour Government was never fully committed to the concept of strengthening Parliament's scrutiny powers. This problem might not have undermined the modernisation agenda had it not been for structural flaws in the machinery set up to implement it. According to Tony Wright MP, the central problem was the Modernisation Committee's failure, at its inception in 1997, to establish a clear aim to be achieved. As a result of the committee's failure to construct a blueprint of what it wanted a scrutinising Parliament to look like, he argues, it was unable to establish a coherent programme to achieve that end.[18] Consequently, it adopted an ad hoc approach to modernisation that became increasingly fuzzy and disconnected. The committee produced reports on a variety of issues – including many 'cosmetic' concerns that Ann Taylor MP had originally dismissed as 'distractions' – in no clear or coherent order. As a result, the modernisation programme did not knit together. Programming of legislation, for instance, could have functioned more effectively had it been explicitly tied to other reforms, such as the increased use of draft Bills and pre-legislative scrutiny – as reformers had always argued it should. But the incoherence of the modernisation programme meant that different aspects of the legislative process became detached, one from another. The result, in the case of programming, is that a tool which should have been part of a broader means of securing better legislation has instead come to be regarded by critics as an end in itself – enabling the government to get its legislation passed swiftly and without obstruction.[19]

The lack of a clear aim was exacerbated by the undue influence that the chair of the Modernisation Committee, the sitting Leader of the House, had over the committee. Without any clear remit or plan of action, the committee's lines of inquiry shifted according to the philosophy and personality of its chair, and although this worked in favour of parliamentary reform when the Leader of the House supported such a course, it hampered such change when the opposite was true. Again, the example of programming is useful in illustrating this point. In December 1998, Margaret Beckett MP replaced Ann Taylor MP as Leader of the House, with the latter becoming Chief Whip. Beckett did not share Taylor's concern for the accountability agenda. She had a clear view that Labour had been given a mandate for implementing its manifesto and believed her prime task, as Leader of the House, was to ensure that the government's legislative programme was passed as easily as possible. 'So programming passed from being a consensual planning instrument to a refinement of the 'guillotine' deplored by parliamentary reformers.'[20] Beckett continued to upset critics, especially on the Conservative benches, with further measures directed at the efficient management of government business, notably the introduction of deferred divisions. Likewise, John Reid MP also upset opposition MPs and reformers generally, by his executive-minded style of Commons leadership. The assertion that: 'I am not here as a parliamentarian. I am here as a Labour politician', provided a strong and, as it transpired, reliable indication of the approach he would follow during his brief chairmanship of the Modernisation Committee.[21]

A groundswell for reform: Sandwiched between Beckett and Reid, however, Robin Cook MP demonstrated that the sword could indeed cut the other way. Replacing Beckett as Commons Leader in 2001, he revitalised the modernisation programme and set out a clearer and more coherent agenda around the objectives of improving Parliament's public image and increasing its capacity to scrutinise the government. It should be said that Cook assumed Leadership of the House at a propitious moment for parliamentary reform. In the space of 12 months prior to his appointment, between 2000 and 2001, two Commissions chaired by Lords Norton and Newton respectively, produced reports outlining clear programmes for reform that constituted a major agenda for change.[22] Furthermore, in 2000, the Liaison Committee of select committee chairs produced an influential report, *Shifting the*

Balance, which – as its title indicated – contained a raft of proposals aimed at reordering the relationship between Parliament and government.[23] It was a significant moment and represented a turning point for the Liaison Committee, which moved from being an essentially administrative body to one that was prepared to champion the rights of Parliament. Although the government rejected almost every proposal contained in its initial report, the dismissive nature of its official response, described by Peter Riddell as 'one of the most oily and evasive documents to emerge from Whitehall in recent years', merely served to stoke the fire of reform.[24] The committee refused to go quietly and revisited its initial report on two further occasions.

In addition to these developments, a landslide victory in the June 2001 general election gave Labour an historic second term in office, with another huge majority, that further contributed to the mood for reform. The composition of the Commons was little changed by the outcome of the election, and the Labour backbenchers – many of whom had previously been criticised for sycophancy – quickly demonstrated a more rebellious streak that was to force the government and the prime minister, in particular, to loosen control over the rank and file. The rejection of the government's attempt to remove Donald Anderson MP and Gwyneth Dunwoody MP from their posts as select committee chairs in summer 2001 illustrated that Labour backbenchers were keen to assert their own, and Parliament's, authority vis a vis the executive. Their determination was shared by the opposition parties. The recommendations of the Norton Commission, which had been set up at the behest of William Hague MP, were adopted by the Conservatives as their blueprint for reform, while Liberal Democrat MPs also expressed their hopes for a stronger Parliament, many joining the cross-party *Parliament First* group of MPs that was formed that year.

Robin Cook's reforms: The prevailing political climate thus constituted a 'window of opportunity', and during two years as Leader of the House Cook successfully piloted a raft of parliamentary reform measures. These included: the establishment of guidelines for core tasks for select committees; the payment of committee chairmen; increased timetabling and greater use of carry-over and pre-legislative scrutiny; the introduction of new media and family-friendly hours; the return of the Commons in September; shorter notice periods for oral questions; and time limits on speeches in the chamber. By the time the bulk of these procedural reforms had been completed, one former Commons clerk wrote to *The Times* to praise them as 'the most systematic package of parliamentary reforms for 100 years. They will enable the House to be far more effective in the passage of legislation and in its scrutiny of the executive, and more relevant to the electorate…As a campaigner for parliamentary reform for more than 40 years, I can now retire happily.'[25]

The programme of modernisation instituted under Cook undoubtedly did more to strengthen Parliament than anything implemented before or since, but it may have been overstating his success to say that reformers could retire happily. Despite the measures that Cook succeeded in getting passed by the Commons, subsequently consolidated under Peter Hain's leadership of the House, the executive remains overwhelmingly dominant. Moreover, it is instructive to contrast the modernisation of the Commons since 1997 with changes implemented in the Lords over the same period. Unlike the Commons, the Lords had no modernisation committee to direct reform of its procedures and practices but nonetheless underwent a significant programme of change after 1997, which developed its capacity to scrutinise legislation in several areas.

A more effective Lords: The Lords expanded the work of their select committees, particularly in relation to scrutiny of matters relating to the European Union, now arguably the most important source of new legislation. In addition to their increased involvement on Lords select committees dealing with European matters, peers now participate much more in Commons standing committees on EU concerns. Furthermore, since 1997, the Economic Affairs and Constitution Committees have been established as sessional committees and the Human Rights Committee as a joint committee. More recently, the Lords set up a Select Committee on the Merits of Statutory Instruments, one of the least effectively scrutinised areas of the legislative process and one where the Commons' machinery is still sorely deficient. The House of Lords has also made greater use of the Grand Committee procedure since 1997, notably in relation to Northern Ireland Orders, which enables increased scrutiny of primary legislation. As Rogers and Walters note, 'Taken alone, none of these changes amounts to "reform" in the traditional sense of the word, but taken collectively, incremental changes such as these have a tremendous effect on what the House does and on the way in which it does it'.[26]

The changes to procedure and practice in the Lords have been more coherent and ordered than the modernisation measures in the Commons, with the effect that the second chamber has arguably improved its ability to scrutinise legislation to a greater degree than the elected body. Consequently, many MPs feel that the Lords, far more than the Commons, effectively interrogates legislation and calls the government to account. Such concerns prompted the *Parliament First* group of MPs, in 2003, to publish a manifesto setting out their agenda for strengthening the legislature.[27] Yet, to date, the group appears to have had little impact and many MPs remain despondent about the state of Parliament and the outcome of the modernisation programme. Indeed, one senior Conservative is so disgruntled about the weakness of the Commons and the perceived negative consequences of modernisation that he recently advocated (only half-jokingly) the creation of a 'Traditionalisation Committee' to roll back every change to parliamentary procedure and practice implemented since 1997.[28]

Such an attitude is too pessimistic. Many reforms since 1997 have been beneficial to Parliament, in terms of increasing its ability to scrutinise government and allowing it to have a greater input into the legislative process. As has been outlined elsewhere in this book, innovations such as the increased use of draft Bills and pre-legislative scrutiny have been widely welcomed, enhancing the role and effectiveness of Parliament and enabling those outside Westminster to engage in the legislative process in a more meaningful way. Likewise, although it is still too early to make any definitive judgement, it appears that the guidelines for core tasks given to select committees have generally had a positive effect, standardising work and making it easier to assess their performance.[29] The use of joint committees is increasing and is improving the interaction between the two Houses, particularly in relation to scrutiny of European issues. More generally, Parliament has seen its scrutiny powers increased in key areas. For instance, the agreement of the prime minister to appear before the Liaison Committee twice a year is an important development, albeit one that was not achieved through the formal modernisation process.

Conclusion: Yet, the terms of trade between Parliament and executive have not shifted decisively. Indeed, in looking back on the process of legislative reform since 1997, there is a sense that, despite some improvements, a major opportunity to reorder the balance of power within Westminster was missed and may not present itself again for many years. Instead of a rapid and substantial transfer of parliamentary power from the executive to the legislature, it seems that any shift in the balance is to be achieved gradually, incrementally and perhaps, above all, very slowly. That is why it is important to keep the reform agenda alive. As this book has highlighted, there is much to be done and much to be learnt: the current system of Private Members' Bills should be reformed to provide individual parliamentarians with a better opportunity to develop their legislative function; standing committees do not perform their role of scrutinising legislation at all effectively and require radical surgery; and delegated legislation, certainly as far as the Commons is concerned, needs to be given far more attention than it currently receives. Consideration should also be given to the establishment of a special committee, comprising representatives from all sides of the House, to plan parliamentary business. Such a business committee would provide a much more transparent and inclusive means of organising the parliamentary agenda, than the current executive-dominated system. The prospect of securing the introduction of such a committee, or indeed any of the reforms mentioned here, is – as ever – constrained by the executive's desire to maintain control.

Yet, as Peter Riddell notes, it would be a mistake to adopt too fatalistic a view of parliamentary reform.[30] The ever-changing political and constitutional context, which is squeezing Westminster out of the political debate, favours neither the executive nor the legislature. As contributors to this publication have shown, the growth of European Union legislation is an area that Parliament has yet to get to grips with, and the increasing impact of human rights issues on British legislation is only now being realised. But constitutional change presents opportunities as well as uncertainties. As several other authors on these pages point out, there are valuable lessons that the Westminster Parliament can learn from the new devolved bodies, particularly in terms of engaging and involving the electorate in the decision making process. It is in the interests of both Parliament and government that Westminster retains its place in the heart of the political system and convinces the public of its importance and worth. That requires a determined effort on behalf of both to address the deficiencies that undermine their effectiveness and devalue each other's reputation. Making the law – one of Parliament's core functions – is an area where improvements can, undoubtedly, be made to the advantage of the legislature and the executive. The practical suggestions for change that this book has outlined will hopefully inform the debate about reform of the legislative process and will encourage both Parliament and government to make this issue a priority in the immediate period.

Endnotes and references:

1   Flinders M. 'Shifting the Balance? Parliament, the Executive and the British Constitution', *Political Studies* (2002) vol.50, p.23.
2   Muylle K. 'Improving the effectiveness of parliamentary legislative procedures', (2003) *Statute Law Review* vol. 24(3), p.170.
3   Avril P. *'Le parlement legislateur'* (1981) RFSP, quoted ibid, p.170.
4   Muylle K., op. cit., p.186.
5   *A Vision for a New Britain* (1997) Labour Party.
6   Quoted in Flinders, op. cit., p.28.
7   HC Deb 14/12/66, vol.738, cols. 480-481.
8   Taylor A. 'New Politics, New Parliament' (1999) quoted in Seaton J. & Winetrobe B. 'Modernising the Commons', (1999) *Political Quarterly* Vol.70(2), p.154.
9   Gay O. *'Modernisation: Making the Commons fit for the twenty-first century'*, in Baldwin N. (ed) *Parliament in the 21st Century* (forthcoming 2005).
10 Quote in Cowley P. 'The Commons: Mr Blair's lapdog?', (October 2001) *Parliamentary Affairs* vol.54(4), p.818; also cited in Gay O., *ibid*.
11 Quoted in Seaton J. and Winetrobe B. op. cit. p.152.
12 Riddell P. *Parliament Under Blair* (2003) argues that this is exactly what happened.
13 Modernisation Committee *The Legislative Process* (1997-98) HC190.
14 Cowley P., op. cit., p.817.
15 In fact, the reformers had hoped that Parliament would adopt a business committee that would allow greater input and agreement between interested parties about the shape and timing of the legislative programme, but this was vetoed by the whips. See Hansard Society *Programming of Legislation* (April 2004) p.6; Gay O., op. cit.
16 Cowley P. & Stuart M. 'Parliament: Mostly continuity, but more change than you'd think' (2001) in Ridley F. & Rush M. (eds) *UK 2001: Into the Second Term* p.272.
17 HC Deb 9/3/98, vol. 308, col.16 cited in Kelso A. 'An invitation to partisanship: The Labour Government, the Modernisation Committee and Efficiency Reforms in the House of Commons' (April 2004) PSA conference paper.
18 Remarks made at a Hansard Society conference on the future of select committees, 4 May 2004, Portcullis House, Westminster. A report of the conference is available on the Hansard Society website (www.hansardsociety.org.uk). See also Wright, T. 'Prospects for Parliamentary Reform', *Parliamentary Affairs* (2004) Vol.57(4).
19 Brazier A. *Programming of Legislation,* Hansard Society briefing paper (April 2004) p.7.
20 Gay O. op. cit.
21 Cited in Robin Cook MP *The Point of Departure* (2003) p.173.
22 *Strengthening Parliament: The Report of the Commission to Strengthen Parliament,* chaired by Lord Norton of Louth, Conservative Party: London (2000).
23 House of Commons Liaison Committee *Shifting the Balance: Select Committees and the Executive* (March 2000) HC300.
24 Riddell P. op. cit., p.248. See also Liaison Committee (1999-2000) *Independence or Control? The Government's to the Committee's First Report – Shifting the Balance: Select Committees and the Executive*, HC748.
25 Ryle M. letter to *The Times,* 5 November 2002.
26 Rogers R. and Walters R. *How Parliament Works* (2004) p.397.
27 Parliament First *Parliament's Last Chance* (2003).
28 Eric Forth MP in interview with Alex Brazier, June 2004.
29 Maer L. & Sandford M. *Select Committees under Scrutiny,* Constitution Unit (2004).
30 Riddell P. op. cit. p.xxi.

Appendix | Key Changes to the Legislative Process 1994-2004

1994

December: Deregulation and Contracting Out Act 1994. The Act established a new form of secondary legislation that allowed ministers to amend or repeal primary legislation that imposed a burden affecting any person carrying on a trade, business or profession. It also introduced a new parliamentary procedure whereby a minister had to consult on a proposal, which would then be laid before Parliament. Separate deregulation committees were set up in both Houses to consider proposals and these committees could suggest amendments before the deregulation order was laid as a formal draft for approval.

1994/5

Implementation of the Jopling Proposals. Reforms included:
- Bills giving effect to the Law Commission's recommendations would be referred to a Second Reading Committee;
- Statutory Instruments subject to the affirmative procedure would generally be referred to a delegated legislation standing committee;
- the government would use best endeavours to avoid late sittings wherever possible, give early notification of recesses and advance notice of the dates of some major debates;
- the House would meet every Wednesday at 10 am (which became 9.30am from 1995-6) and hold timed adjournment debates decided by ballot, until 2.00pm;
- Private Members' Bills would be confined to Fridays.

1997

May: General election; Labour Government elected.

Establishment of the Select Committee on Modernisation of the House of Commons. The committee was set up to consider how the practices and procedures of the House should be modernised and to make recommendations.

July: Publication of the Modernisation Committee's report *'The Legislative Process'* (HC 190). The report puts forward a series of proposals including the introduction of the programming of Bills (i.e. the imposition of a timetable for the Bills' Commons passage following Second Reading), pre-legislative scrutiny of Bills, explanatory notes and the carry-over of Bills from one parliamentary session to another.

November: Adoption of the report *'The Legislative Process'.* Implementation of a series of reforms, including:
- programme motions to be agreed on a number of Bills including Northern Ireland Elections, Government of Wales and Criminal Justice Act;
- draft Bills to be considered by select committees. Early examples included draft Bills on pension splitting on divorce and limited liability partnerships.

December: Explanatory Material for Bills. It was agreed that explanatory notes would accompany Bills from the 1998-99 parliamentary session onwards.

1998

March: Publication of the Modernisation Committee's report *'Carry-Over of Bills'* (HC 543). The report recommended that, in certain defined circumstances, it should be possible to carry over a Bill to complete its remaining stages in the following session.

June: Carry-over of Public Bills. The House agreed to carry-over the Financial Services and Markets Bill.

Procedures in the Chamber. Several reforms were agreed, including:
- extra time to be allowed for interventions in short speeches;
- the Speaker was given discretion to impose a variable time limit on speeches.

The Scrutiny of European Business. Reforms were agreed, including:
- changing the European Legislation Committee's name to the European Scrutiny Committee;
- the Scrutiny Committee should conduct an experiment in pre- and post-Council scrutiny;
- the establishment of three separate European Standing committees;
- Standing Orders were amended to enable departmental select committees to be more closely involved with European business.

December: The Parliamentary Calendar. Changes to the parliamentary calendar were agreed; for an experimental period it was decided that the House would meet 11.30am - 7.00pm on Thursdays.

1999

The Procedure Committee issues a series of reports on *'The Procedural Consequences of Devolution.'* The report's recommendations included that once devolved government was in place the range and details of questions to be put to the Secretaries of State for Scotland and Wales should be reduced to matters relating to their ministerial responsibilities and that the select committees on Scotland and Wales should remain in place.

May: Sittings of the House in Westminster Hall. The House established a parallel chamber, which would meet in the Grand Committee Room, Westminster Hall.

July: Scottish Parliament and the Welsh Assembly. The Scottish Parliament and Welsh Assembly were officially opened and took up their full powers.

Thursday Sittings. The House agreed that the Thursday sitting hours would be continued for a further session.

November: House of Lords Act. The Act removed the rights of most hereditary peers to sit in the Lords. The 'Weatherill Amendment' allowed 92 hereditary peers to remain and keep voting rights until the next stage of reform was concluded.

2000

January: Publication of *A House for The Future,* Report of the Royal Commission on Reform of the House of Lords, Chaired by Rt Hon Lord Wakeham, (Cm 4534). The report recommended that a reformed chamber should consist of 550 members with the majority being appointed by an independent Appointments Commission, the remainder being elected.

March: Publication of the Liaison Committee's report, *'Shifting the Balance; Select Committees and the Executive'* (HC 300). The report made proposals to improve the operation of select committees. The report also highlighted the importance of pre-legislative scrutiny in the work of select committees.

Publication of the Procedure Committee's report *'Delegated Legislation'* (HC 48). The report strongly criticised the system for scrutinising delegated legislation and supported, with minor modifications, the package of reforms laid out in the 1996 Procedure Committee report on the same subject.

July: Publication of the Modernisation Committee's report *'Programming of Legislation and Timing of Votes'* **(HC 589).** The report made a number of recommendations to extend the use of programming for government Bills even in the absence of cross-party support for such programming.

October: Implementation of the Human Rights Act 1998. The Act gave effect to rights guaranteed under the European Convention on Human Rights. Section 19 of the Act contained provisions requiring a Minister to make a statement in relation to each Bill about its compatibility with human rights legislation. The Act also allowed ministers to make a new form of delegated legislation known as Remedial Orders. This enabled the UK courts to find that a provision in an Act was incompatible with the HRA, and could therefore be used to amend primary legislation. Subsequently, a Joint Committee on Human Rights was established and met for the first time in January 2001. The Committee's remit was to consider and to report on matters relating to human rights in the United Kingdom (but excluding consideration of individual cases) and proposals for remedial orders and draft remedial orders.

November: Changes to programming procedures: New arrangements were adopted for programme orders to set out a timetable for the conclusion of proceedings on a Bill. The new arrangements reduced the amount of time normally available for debate on programme motions. The House of Commons approved the Modernisation Committee's report on the programming of legislation and timing of votes. It was agreed that deferred divisions, for certain forms of business such as motions on Statutory Instruments, should be introduced in the 2000-01 Session.

2001

April: Publication of the Modernisation Committee's report *'Programming of Legislation'* **(HC 382).** The programming report urged greater use of programming procedures and recognised the abandonment of the previously consensual approach to programming.

Regulatory Reform Act 2001. An extension of the Deregulation and Contracting Out Act 1994 was enacted. It widened cover to burdens affecting persons in the carrying on of any activity and introduced a power to make subordinate provisions, a further form of delegated legislation.

June: General Election. Labour Government re-elected. Sessional Orders were reconfirmed, in a slightly modified form, giving more powers to the programming committees and programming sub-committees. These Orders limited proceedings in the committee, or sub-committee, to two hours and reduced the amount of time normally available for debate on programme motions.

2002

February: Publication of the Procedure Committee report *'Making Remedial Orders: Recommendations by the Joint Committee on Human Rights'* (HC 626). The report backed the recommendations of the Joint Committee on Human Rights in its report on 'remedial orders', which made procedures for the greater degree of scrutiny in the case of the 'super-affirmative' form of delegated legislation.

May: The Commons adopted guidelines for core functions and duties to be carried out by select committees. These functions include conducting scrutiny of any published draft Bill within the committee's responsibilities, and the establishment of a scrutiny unit to provide resources and support for select committees undertaking pre-legislative scrutiny.

October: Publication of the Modernisation Committee report, *Modernisation of the House of Commons: A Reform Programme* (HC 224). The report recommended reforms including an increase in the number of Bills published in draft for pre-legislative scrutiny, amendment of Standing Orders to permit carry-over of Bills from one session to the next and the development of arrangements for consultation with opposition parties on the broad shape of the legislative year. The report also proposed changes to the hours and calendar of Commons sittings.

2003

June: The House of Lords agreed to establish the Merits of Statutory Instruments Select Committee with effect from the beginning of 2003-04 session.

In the House of Commons, a new Standing Order was established to permit written ministerial statements.

Payment for Chairmen of Select Committees: The House agreed that the chairmen of select committees should be paid an extra £12,000 per annum.

November: The House resolved to continue in the next session of Parliament the order relating to the programming of Bills made by the House on 28 June 2001 and programme orders of the current session of Parliament relating to Bills.

2004

July: The Procedure Committee report *'Programming of Legislation'* (HC 325). The report observed the problems with programming, including its lack of cross-party support. It recommended that programming motions should be decided without debate only where there is cross-party support; on other occasions the government would, if necessary, have to justify such a motion in a one hour debate. In exchange, the committee would expect parties to adopt a constructive approach to programming.

October: Publication of the Procedure Committee report *The Government's Response to the Committee's Fourth Report,* (HC 1169). The Government did not accept the proposal that programme motions should only be decided without debate if there was cross-party support for the motion, or, if such support was not forthcoming, that the Government would have to justify the motion in a one-hour debate.

Changes to procedures: The Government introduced changes to Commons Standing Orders which had the effect of making permanent the basic system of programming in operation since 2001. At the same time, the use of deferred divisions was made permanent and the provisions allowing Bills to be carried over into the following session were confirmed in Standing Orders.

Publication of House of Lords Constitution Committee report, *Parliament and the Legislative Process,* (HL 173-1). The report made a number of recommendations including; that the Government should publish Bills in draft unless there was a compelling reason not to do so; the Government and Commons Liaison Committee (with input from the Lords) should decide which draft Bills should be subject to pre-legislative scrutiny; every Bill at some stage be subject to scrutiny by a committee empowered to take evidence. The Committee emphasised the importance of both Government and Parliament monitoring Acts through post-legislative scrutiny.

Glossary

Act: A law passed by Parliament.

Bill: A proposal for a new law which is debated by both Houses of Parliament. A Bill may be introduced into either House, apart from money Bills which the Lords cannot initiate or amend. A Bill becomes an Act when it has received the Royal Assent.

Cabinet: The team of MPs and Peers appointed by the prime minister responsible for running departments of state and deciding government policy.

Committee Stage: The stage when a Bill is considered line-by-line, clause-by-clause and amendments are made.

Committee of the Whole House: If a Bill is considered of great constitutional importance, or if a very fast passage through Parliament is required, then the whole House may act as the committee that examines the Bill after Second Reading.

Constituency: A geographical area of the country represented by an MP. The population of this area are known as constituents. There are currently 659 constituencies in the UK.

Consultation Document: Outline of a new policy put out by a government department. Members of the public and experts are invited to give their views.

Debate: A discussion that takes place between MPs or Peers which may end in a vote.

Deferred Divisions: MPs are able to vote on a range of business days after the actual event has taken place.

Delegated (or Secondary) Legislation: Law made by ministers under powers deriving from Acts of Parliament. They enable the government to make changes to the law without having to introduce a whole new Act of Parliament.

Early Day Motions (EDMs): MPs can sign this printed statement showing their support for an issue at hand and calling for government action.

First Reading: The title of a Bill is read out and copies of it are printed, but no debate takes place.

Free Vote: In a free vote, MPs are allowed to vote as they wish and are not under instruction from their parties' whips. Free votes are most often granted on issues of conscience.

Green Paper: A consultation document introducing policy proposals.

Government: Headed by the prime minister, the government introduces the majority of laws considered by Parliament.

Hansard: The official transcript of Parliament which is published daily and put on the parliamentary website.

House of Commons: The elected House of the UK legislature, made up of Members of Parliament. This House is the more powerful of the two Houses of Parliament.

House of Lords: Sometimes known as the Upper House of the legislature. It is composed of unelected members; like the Commons its functions include passing legislation and holding government to account.

Lords Stages: A Bill is sent for its Lords Stages after it has received its Third Reading (in the Commons). The House of Lords considers the Bill and can make revisions.

Member of Parliament (MP): An elected representative who sits in the House of Commons.

Minister: MPs or Peers who lead or assist in one of the government departments. Most departments have several ministers, led by a Secretary of State who sits in the Cabinet.

Opposition: The second largest political party in Parliament forms the Official Opposition. All parties other than the government are considered the opposition.

Parliament Acts: The Parliament Acts of 1911 and 1949 restrict the power of the House of Lords to block legislation introduced by the government. If the Lords refuse to agree to a Bill which has already been approved by the Commons, the government can pass the Bill into law, after a delay of one year, without the Lords agreement.

Parliamentary Questions: Asked by MPs or Peers to the relevant Minister to find out detail of government activity. There are two types of questions: oral and written.

Peer: A member of the House of Lords.

Pre-legislative Scrutiny: Involves a general inquiry or more recently the issuing of a draft Bill to be considered by a parliamentary committee. It includes scrutiny of consultative documents, Green Papers and White Papers.

Prime Minister: The Prime Minister is the head of the government and is the leader of the political party that has most seats in the House of Commons.

Prime Minister's Question Time: Every Wednesday at 12pm, when the House is sitting, the Prime Minister answers questions from MPs about the work of the government.

Private Bills: Proposals for legislation affecting the powers of particular bodies (such as local authorities) or involving plans relating to areas such as railways, roads and harbours, which are subject to a special form of parliamentary procedure.

Private Members' Bill: Proposal for legislation introduced by an individual MP or Peer.

Programming of Legislation: In the Commons, programming involves the imposition of a timetable for the passage of a Bill immediately after Second Reading. There is no programming in the Lords.

Public Bills: Bills that change the general law, which make up by far the most significant part of the parliamentary legislative process.

Queen's Speech: Annual announcement by the Queen of the Bills that the government intends to put before Parliament in the forthcoming session.

Report Stage: Major debate when changes that have been made at committee stage are looked at. Considerations for further amendment can also be suggested.

Royal Assent: The final stage of legislation when the Royal Seal of approval is formally given and a Bill becomes an Act.

Second Reading: When the general principles of a Bill are debated in each House for the first time.

Select Committees: In both Houses, select committees are charged with scrutinising government activity. They are composed of MPs or Peers from different parties. They can call on ministers, civil servants or outside bodies to submit information for reports and investigations and produce reports with recommendations for government action.

Shadow Cabinet: The group of shadow ministers from the chief opposition party, the majority of whom would form the government if their party came into power after a general election.

Speaker of the House of Commons: The Speaker chairs debates in the main Commons chamber, selects members to speak and maintains order.

Special Standing Committee: After second reading a Bill may be committed to a Special Standing Committee which though nominated like a standing committee, acts for four sittings like a select committee (i.e. hearing evidence from interested parties) and thereafter going through the Bill in the same way as a normal standing committee.

Statute Law: Consists of Acts of Parliament - primary legislation - and delegated or secondary legislation made by ministers under powers given to them by an Act.

Standing Committee: Scrutinises Bills in details in the Commons, following Second Reading. There are no standing committees in the Lords. The standing committee is made up of between 18 and 40 MPs and its membership always reflects the relative strengths of the parties in the Commons.

Third Reading: The House takes an overview of the Bill as finally amended and provides a final opportunity for debating a Bill in its amended form.

Whips: MPs and peers who coordinate business in Parliament, and who try to ensure that backbench members of their party vote with the leadership.

White Paper: A statement of government policy that may precede a Bill. There may also have been an earlier consultation document (Green Paper) on the same subject.

Bibliography

Allen, G., *The Last Prime Minister; Being Honest About the UK Presidency* (2001) Imprint Academic: Thorverton

Blackburn, R., & Kennon, A., *Parliament: Functions, Practice and Procedures. Second Edition* (2003) Sweet and Maxwell: London

Brazier, A., *Systematic Scrutiny* (2000) Hansard Society: London

Brazier, A., *Parliament at the Apex* (2003a) Hansard Society: London

Brazier, A., *Issues in Law Making, Briefing Paper 1: Private Members' Bills* (2003b) Hansard Society: London

Brazier, A., *Issues in Law Making, Briefing Paper 2: Standing Committees,* (2003c) Hansard Society: London

Brazier, A., *Issues in Law Making, Briefing Paper 3: Delegated Legislation* (2003d) Hansard Society: London

Brazier, A., *Issues in Law Making, Briefing Paper 4, Programming of Legislation* (2004a) Hansard Society: London

Brazier, A., *Issues in Law Making, Briefing Paper 5: Pre-Legislative Scrutiny* (2004b) Hansard Society: London

Brazier, R., *Ministers of the Crown* (1997) Clarendon: Oxford

Burrows, N., *Devolution* (2000) Sweet and Maxwell: London

Butler, D., Adonis, A., & Travers, T., *Failure in British Government, The Politics of the Poll Tax* (1994) Oxford University Press: Oxford

Coleman, S., & Norman, E., *New Media and Social Inclusion* (2000) Hansard Society: London

Commission to Strengthen Parliament, *Strengthening Parliament* (2000) Conservative Party

Cook, R., *Point of Departure* (2003) Simon and Schuster: London

Crossman, R., *The Crossman Diaries. The Diary of a Cabinet Minister Volume 3* (1977) Hamilton: London

Dainith, T. & Page, A., *The Executive in the Constitution* (2000) Oxford University Press: Oxford

Erskine May., *Parliamentary Practice*, 23rd Edition (2004) Butterworths: London

Flinders, M., 'Shifting the Balance? Parliament, the Executive and the British Constitution,' *Political Studies* (2002) Vol.50

Griffith, J.A.G., & Ryle, M., *Parliament, Functions, Practice and Procedures* (1989) Sweet and Maxwell: London

Hansard Society, *Making the Law*: The Report of the Hansard Society Commission on the Legislative Process (1992) Hansard Society: London

Hansard Society, *The Challenge for Parliament: Making Government Accountable,* Report of the Hansard Society Commission on Parliamentary Scrutiny (2001) Vacher Dod: London

Hayhurst, J.D., & Wallington, P., *'The Parliamentary Scrutiny of Delegated Legislation'* (1998) in Zander, M., The Law Making Process, Fourth edition (1994) Butterworth: London

Himsworth, C., & O'Neill, C., *Scotland's constitution: law and practice* (2003) LexisNexisUK: Edinburgh

Jowell, J., & Oliver, D., (eds), *The Changing Constitution,* Fifth edition, Clarendon: Oxford

Judge, D., 'Whatever Happened to Parliamentary Democracy in the United Kingdom?', *Parliamentary Affairs* (2004) Vol. 57, No. 3

Kennon, A., 'Pre-legislative Scrutiny of Draft Bills,' *Public Law* (Autumn 2004) Stevens: London

Lynch, P., *Scottish Government and Politics: An Introduction* (2001) Edinburgh University Press: Edinburgh

Marsh, D., & Read, M., *Private Members' Bills* (1988) Cambridge University Press

McFadden, J., & Lazarowicz, M., *The Scottish Parliament,* Third edition (2003) T&T Clark: Edinburgh

Norton, P., (ed) *Legislatures* (1990) Oxford University Press: Oxford

Norton, P., *Does Parliament Matter?* (1993) Harvester Wheatsheaf: London

Page, E.C., *Governing by Numbers: Delegated Legislation and Everyday Policy-Making* (2001) Hart Publishing: Portland

Parliament First, *Parliament's Last Chance* (2003) Parliament First: London

Power, G., *Parliamentary Scrutiny of Draft Legislation:1997-1999* (2000) The Constitution Unit, University College: London

Rawlings, R., *Delineating Wales – Constitutional, Legal, and Administrative Aspects of National Devolution* (2003) University of Wales

Rhodes, R.A.W., & Dunleavy, P. (eds) *Prime Minister, Cabinet and the Core Executive* (1995) Macmillan: London

Riddell, P., *Parliament Under Blair* (2000) Politicos Publishing: London

Rogers, R., & Walters, R., *How Parliament Works, Fifth Edition* (2004) Pearson Education Limited: Essex

Rush, M., & Ettinghausen, C., *Opening Up the Usual Channels* (2002) Hansard Society: London

Seaton, J. & Winetrobe, B., 'Modernising the Commons', *Political Quarterly*, (1999) v.70

Silk, P., & Walters, R., *How Parliament Works,* Fourth Edition), (1998) Addisson Welsey Longman Limited: Essex

Smith-Hughes, A., *Parliament, the City and Financial Regulation; A Review of the Passage of the Financial Services and Markets Act 2000* (2001) Hansard Society: London

Taylor, A., 'New Politics, New Parliament' (1996) (speech given on May 14, 1996)

Tyrie, A., *Mr Blair's Poodle: An Agenda for Reviving the House of Commons* (2000) Centre for Policy Studies: London

Weir, S. & Beetham, D., *Political Power and Democratic Control in Britain* (1999) Routledge: London

Winetrobe, B K., *Realising the Vision of a Parliament with a Purpose: An Audit of the First Year of Scottish Parliament* (2001) Constitution Unit: UCL

Wright, T. (ed) *The British Political Process* (2000) Routledge: London

Zander, M., *The Law Making Process*, Fourth Edition (1994) Butterworths: London

Government and Parliamentary Publications

Foreign & Commonwealth Office (2003) *Implementation of EU Legislation: An Independent Study of the Foreign and Commonwealth Office by Mr Robin Bellis*, Clifford Chance

Constitution Committee, House of Lords (2003) Second report, *Devolution: inter-institutional relations in the UK,* HL 147

Constitution Committee, House of Lords (2003-4) *Parliament and the Legislative Process,* HL 173-I

European Scrutiny Committee, House of Commons (2001-02) Thirteenth report, *European Scrutiny in the Commons,* HC 152

European Scrutiny Committee, House of Commons (2001-02) *Scrutiny of European Matters in the House of Commons: Government memorandum from the Leader of the House of Commons,* HC 508

European Scrutiny Committee, House of Commons (2003-04) *Eighth report, The Committee's Work in 2003,* HC 42

European Union Committee, House of Lords (2002-03) First report, *Review of Scrutiny of European Legislation,* HL 15

Cabinet Office (1997) *A Voice for Wales* (White Paper), Cm 3718

Cabinet Office (2003) *Transposition Guide: How to Implement European Directives Effectively*

Cabinet Office (January 2004) *The Government's Response to the Report of the Joint Committee on the Draft Civil Contingencies Bill,* Cm 6078

Home Affairs Committee, House of Commons (2002-03) *Criminal Justice Bill*, HC 83

House of Commons Information Office (2003) *House of Commons Factsheet Series No.1 Parliamentary Stages of a Government Bill*

House of Commons Library Research Paper (1996) *Special Standing Committees in Both Houses,* 96/14

House of Commons Library Research Paper (1997) *Aspects of Parliamentary Reform,* 97/64

House of Commons Library Research Paper (1997) *Parliamentary Reform: The Commons Modernisation Programme,* 97/107

House of Commons Library Research Paper (2000) *Shifting Control? Aspects of the Executive-Parliamentary Relationship,* 00/92

House of Commons Library Research Paper (2002) *The Enterprise Bill,* 02/21

Liaison Committee, House of Commons (1999-2000) *Shifting the Balance: Select Committees and the Executive,* HC 300

Liaison Committee, House of Commons (1999-2000) *Independence or Control,* HC 748

Liaison Committee, House of Commons (2003-04) *Annual Report for 2003,* HC 446

Merits of Statutory Instruments Committee (2003-04) *Special Report: The Committee's Methods of Working,* HL Paper 73

Modernisation Committee, House of Commons (1997-98) *The Legislative Process,* HC 190

Modernisation Committee, House of Commons (1997-98) *Explanatory Material for Bills,* HC 389

Modernisation Committee, House of Commons (1997-98) *Carry Over of Public Bills,* HC 543

Modernisation Committee, House of Commons (1998-99) *First report, The Parliamentary Calendar: Initial Proposals,* HC 60

Modernisation Committee, House of Commons (1999-2000) First report, *Programming of Legislation and Timing of Votes,* HC 589

Modernisation Committee, House of Commons (2001-02) *Modernisation of the House of Commons: A reform programme,* HC 1168

Modernisation Committee, House of Commons (2002-03) *Programming of Bills,* HC 1222

Modernisation Committee, House of Commons (2004) *Connecting Parliament with the Public,* HC 368

Procedure Committee, House of Commons (1984-85) *Public Bill Procedure,* HC 49-1

Procedure Committee, House of Commons (1985-86) *Allocation of Time to Government Bills in Standing Committees,* HC 324.

Procedure Committee, House of Commons (1994-95) *Private Member's Bills,* HC 38

Procedure Committee, House of Commons (1995-96) *Delegated Legislation,* HC 152

Procedure Committee, House of Commons (1999–2000) *Delegated Legislation,* HC 48

Procedure Committee, House of Commons (1999-2000) *Programming of Legislation and Timing of Votes,* HC 589

Procedure Committee, House of Commons (2002-03) *Delegated Legislation: Proposals for a Sifting Committee,* HC 50

Procedure Committee, House of Commons (2002-03) Delegated Legislation: *Proposals for a Sifting Committee - The Government's Response to the Committee's First Report,* HC 684.

Procedure Committee, House of Commons (2002-03) *Procedures for Debates, Private Members' Bills and the Powers of the Speaker,* HC 333

Procedure Committee, House of Commons (2002-03) *Procedures for Debates, Private Members' Bills and the Powers of the Speaker: The Government's Response to the Committee's Fourth Report of Session 2002-03,* HC 610

Procedure Committee, House of Commons (2003-04) *Programming of Legislation,* HC 325

Procedure Committee, House of Commons (2003-04) *The Government's Response to the Committee's Fourth Report,* HC 1169

Public Administration Committee, House of Commons (2004) *A Draft Civil Service Bill, Completing the Reform,* HC 128-1

Royal Commission on the Reform of the House of Lords (2000) *A House for the Future,* chaired by Lord Wakeham, CM 4534

Sittings of the House Committee, House of Commons (1991-92) *Select Committee on Sittings of the House,* HC 20-I

Scottish Office (1999) *Shaping Scotland's Parliament,* Stationery Office: Edinburgh

Welsh Affairs Committee (2002-3) Fourth report, *The Primary Legislative Process as it affects Wales,* HC 79

Welsh Affairs Committee (2002-3) *The Government's Response to the Fourth Report of the Committee: the Primary Legislative Process as it affects Wales,* HC 989

Wiseman, H.V. (ed) (1966) *Parliament and the Executive,* London: Routledge and Kegan Paul

Further publications from the HANSARD SOCIETY

Making the Law: The Report of the Hansard Society Commission on the Legislative Process
(ISBN 0 900432 24 1), £16, 1992

An authoritative text on the UK legislative process whose recommendations have been extremely influential within Parliament and government.

Parliamentary Affairs - Special Edition
Edited by Declan McHugh and F.F. Ridley
(ISSN 0031 2290) £9, October 2004

Reflections on British Parliamentary Democracy.

A 60th anniversary special issue of *Parliamentary Affairs* published in October 2004 at the discounted price of £9.00. Contributors include David Butler, Dawn Oliver and Peter Kellner.

An Audit of Political Engagement
(ISBN 1 904363 38 5), Free of charge, March 2004

Hansard Society/Electoral Commission report auditing the nature & extent of the UK public's political engagement.

Parliament at the Apex: Parliamentary scrutiny and regulatory bodies
(Alex Brazier) (ISBN 0 900 432 96 9), £7.50, February 2003
Looking at Parliament's relationship with regulatory bodies.

Opening Up the Usual Channels
(Michael Rush and Clare Ettinghausen)
(ISBN 0 900 432 86 1), £10, December 2002
Based on original research into the people, personalities and systems that organise business in Parliament.

Paying for Politics
(ISBN 0 900 432 76 4), £1, August 2002
Looking at the principles of funding political parties.

Parliament, the City and Financial Regulation
(ISBN 0 900 432 0 1), £10, October 2001
A review of the passage of the Financial Services and Markets Act 2000.

The Challenge for Parliament: Making Government Accountable:
Report of the Hansard Society Commission on Parliamentary Scrutiny
(ISBN 0 900 5702 31X), £35 June 2001
An influential text which analyses Parliament's scrutiny functions and makes recommendations to improve the way that Parliament holds government to account.

Publications can be ordered from:
hansard@hansard.lse.ac.uk
or by fax 020 7395 4008
or by post from Hansard Society, 9 Kingsway, London WC2B 6XF.